The Ultimate Guide to Buying a Business Under 100K

A Step by Step Guide to Buying Your First Business Venture

Darkblue Wells

Table of Contents

Introduction	1
Introduction to Small Business Acquisition	5
Why Buy an Existing Business?	6
Overview of Affordable Business Opportunities	9
Closing Remarks	12
Researching Viable Business Opportunities	14
Where to find businesses for sale	15
Evaluating industry trends and market demand	17
Bringing It All Together	21
Assessing Financial Health	23
Reviewing Financial Statements	24
Understanding Key Financial Ratios	27
Concluding Thoughts	30
Due Diligence	32
Legal Considerations and Contracts	33
Evaluating Operational Strengths and Weaknesses	37
Summary and Reflections	42
Valuing a Business	44
Methods of Business Valuation	45
Negotiation Strategies for Final Pricing	48
Insights and Implications	52
Securing Financing	53
Traditional vs. Alternative Financing	54
Leveraging Seller Financing Opportunities	58
Final Insights	61
Closing the Deal	63
Preparing Closing Documents	64
Managing the Transition Effectively	67

Final Thoughts	70
Post-Purchase Integration	72
Onboarding Employees and Clients	73
Implementing Operational Changes	76
Final Thoughts	82
Case Studies and Success Stories	84
Successful Acquisition Under $100K	85
Lessons Learned and Key Takeaways	89
Final Thoughts	93
Ongoing Management and Growth	95
Continuous Improvement Strategies	96
Expanding Your Business Sustainably	101
Final Thoughts	104
Conclusion	106
Recap of the Journey and Emphasizing Due Diligence	107
Real-World Application and Long-Term Vision	112
Bringing It All Together	117

Chapter 1
Introduction

Did you know that nearly 16 million small businesses in the U.S. are classified as "micro" enterprises, often available for under $100,000? This stunning statistic highlights a golden opportunity, especially for those of us who have always harbored dreams of owning a business. The prospect of becoming your own boss might seem like an elusive fantasy, a privilege reserved for the wealthy or extraordinarily lucky. However, the reality couldn't be further from that notion.

Imagine this: one day, you walk into your favorite café, the aroma of freshly brewed coffee enveloping you. Only this time, it's not just a place where you enjoy your morning ritual; it's your café. You greet regular customers by name, you've designed the menu, and every success feels deeply personal. Now, consider that this dream could become a reality for less than the cost of a new car. How empowering is that?

Buying an existing business offers numerous benefits that make it an attractive option over starting from scratch. When you purchase an established business, you're stepping into a tried-and-true system with existing customers, brand recognition, and operational processes already in place. You're not starting at zero; you're accelerating from a running start. As one seasoned entrepreneur put it, "I didn't just buy a business; I gained a community." This sense of community fosters immediate support and provides a solid foundation upon which to build and grow.

Yet, despite these advantages, many people hesitate to embark on this journey due to common misconceptions. One such myth is that buying a small business requires a significant amount of capital. In reality, with the right resources and knowledge, even a modest budget can unlock incredible potential. As one savvy buyer shared, "With the right approach and an informed strategy, navigating the complexities of business acquisition is entirely within reach."

This book serves as your comprehensive roadmap, designed to guide you through a structured, 10-step process that covers everything from discovery to successful integration. Each chapter delves into essential aspects of the business buying journey, ensuring you won't miss any critical detail along the way. By following this well-crafted framework, you'll find yourself well-equipped to handle the challenges and reap the rewards of small business ownership. "Navigating this journey transformed my life, and I want to share how it can do the same for you," echoes the sentiment of many who've walked this path before.

So, take a moment to reflect on your personal motivations and aspirations. Why do you want to become a business owner? Is it the allure of financial independence, the desire to create something meaningful, or perhaps the flexibility to design your own work-life balance? Whatever your reasons, they are the fuel that will drive you forward on this entrepreneurial journey.

Envision where you want to be five years from now. Picture yourself at the helm of your small enterprise, experiencing the satisfaction of seeing your hard work come to fruition. "The journey of a thousand miles begins with a single step, and this book will help you take that step confidently into small business ownership."

The world of business acquisition is not filled with insurmountable barriers but rather with inviting gateways waiting to be crossed. Many have embarked on this journey and found it rewarding, fulfilling, and yes, profitable. With millions of micro-enterprises available for relatively affordable prices, why shouldn't you be next? This is not just another business book. It's a guide to transforming your aspirations into tangible outcomes, a testament to the power of informed decisions and strategic planning.

As you delve deeper into the chapters ahead, you will encounter practical advice, real-life examples, and actionable steps tailored to demystify the process of buying a small business. You'll learn how to identify promising opportunities, evaluate their worth, secure financing, negotiate terms, and integrate seamlessly into your newly acquired business. We'll also tackle the emotional and psychological aspects, preparing you to navigate the ups and downs with resilience and optimism.

Ultimately, this book aims to empower you to make savvy business decisions that align with your goals and values. It's about equipping you with the tools needed to turn the concept of business ownership from a distant dream into a vibrant reality. As you turn each page, think of it as an investment in your future, laying the groundwork for a journey that could redefine your life in extraordinary ways.

Take a deep breath. This is the beginning of a thrilling adventure, one where you're in the driver's seat. Armed with the insights and strategies contained within these pages, you're ready to explore the landscape of small business acquisition with confidence and clarity. Imagine the possibilities that lie ahead—new challenges, triumphs, and the profound satisfaction that comes from taking control of your professional destiny.

Welcome to your entrepreneurial journey. Let's make that dream of owning a business not just a possibility, but a reality. With determination, the right guidance, and a clear roadmap, your goal of becoming a business owner is not just achievable—it's imminent. So, let's get started!

Chapter 2
Introduction to Small Business Acquisition

Acquiring a small business is an exciting and strategic move for aspiring entrepreneurs. It offers a plethora of opportunities to step into the world of business ownership without starting from scratch. Buying an existing business under $100,000 can present several advantages, making it a viable path towards achieving financial independence and entrepreneurial success. Whether it's inheriting an established customer base or leveraging the operational frameworks already in place, this approach can significantly reduce risks and accelerate profitability. Readers will find that understanding these fundamental aspects of small business acquisition can pave the way for a more informed and confident decision-making process.

In this chapter, we will explore the core benefits of purchasing an existing small business, highlighting the immediate rewards and long-term potential it holds. We will delve into the critical factors that set acquired businesses apart, such as the value of an established customer base, the seamless transition afforded by pre-existing operational structures, and the inherent brand recognition that comes with the territory. Beyond these initial advantages, we'll also look at the prospects for growth and scalability that savvy new owners can harness to elevate their ventures. By the end of this chapter, readers will possess a clear understanding of why investing in an existing business can be a more secure and rewarding pathway compared to launching a new one from the ground up.

Why Buy an Existing Business?

When considering the advantages of purchasing an existing small business, it is essential to recognize the immediate and tangible benefits that such acquisitions offer. Buying an established business, especially one under $100,000, can provide a stable foundation for new ownership, reduce inherent risks, and expedite profitability. This section delves into these benefits, helping readers make well-informed decisions.

One of the most significant advantages of acquiring an existing business is the established customer base. Starting a new venture often involves immense effort and resources to attract and retain customers. However, buying an already operational business means inheriting its loyal clientele. This pre-existing customer network ensures a steady stream of revenue from day one, significantly reducing the uncertainty and time needed to build a customer base from scratch. For instance, imagine purchasing a local bakery that has been serving the community for over a decade. The regular customers who have grown accustomed to the bakery's products and services provide immediate financial stability, allowing the new owner to focus on maintaining and expanding the business rather than investing in customer acquisition. This advantage cannot be overstated, as it sets the tone for long-term success and growth.

In addition to an established customer base, an operational framework is another critical benefit of buying an existing business. Starting a business from scratch requires developing processes, systems, and hiring staff, which can be both time-consuming and costly. Conversely, an existing business comes with well-established operational procedures and experienced employees. These operational frameworks streamline the transition for new owners and ensure business continuity. For example, acquiring a small manufacturing company with robust production processes and supplier relationships allows the new owner to focus on optimizing efficiency rather than reinventing the wheel. This seamless transition is invaluable, providing a head start that can lead to quicker profitability and reduced operational headaches.

Brand recognition also plays a pivotal role in the success of an acquired business. Building brand awareness and credibility from the ground up is a daunting task, often requiring substantial marketing efforts and expenditure. On the other hand, purchasing a business with an established brand allows buyers to leverage existing market presence and reputation. This benefit translates into immediate consumer trust and reduces the risk of market rejection. Take, for example, the scenario of buying a boutique clothing store known for its high-quality products and excellent customer service. The store's existing brand equity ensures that customers familiar with the brand remain loyal, aiding in smoother market entry and saving costs on branding initiatives. This inherent trust can be a powerful tool in driving sales and fostering growth.

Another compelling advantage of acquiring an existing business is the potential for growth. Many existing businesses possess untapped opportunities for scalability and improvement. New owners can capitalize on these opportunities by implementing innovative strategies and operational enhancements. For instance, a business that has not yet embraced digital marketing or e-commerce could experience substantial growth by tapping into online sales channels. Additionally, improving product quality, diversifying offerings, or expanding to new markets are strategies that can increase profitability. The potential for growth is particularly appealing because it allows new owners to introduce fresh perspectives and drive the business toward greater success. This untapped potential represents a golden opportunity for visionary entrepreneurs willing to inject new life into existing operations.

These advantages underscore why purchasing an existing business can be a more secure and rewarding path compared to starting from scratch. The established customer base provides immediate revenue and stability, while the operational framework simplifies the transition process. Leveraging brand recognition offers a market edge, and the potential for growth presents limitless possibilities for new owners. Together, these factors create a robust platform for entrepreneurial success.

Overview of Affordable Business Opportunities

Understanding the variety of small businesses available for purchase under $100,000 can open a world of opportunities for aspiring entrepreneurs. By exploring different sectors and types of businesses, potential buyers can find an option that aligns with their skills, interests, and financial capacity. This section will delve into several promising categories that often fall within this price range, providing insights to encourage readers to explore their options further.

Service-Based Industries are a considerable sector where many affordable businesses can be found. These businesses typically require lower start-up costs and overheads, making them an attractive option for first-time business owners. Examples include cleaning services, consulting firms, home repair services, and mobile car detailing. The low inventory requirements and reduced need for physical space contribute to keeping initial investments manageable. Additionally, service-based businesses often benefit from recurring revenue models, which can provide a steady and predictable income stream.

Franchises offer another appealing option for those looking to buy a business with less risk and more support. Entry-level franchises can often be acquired for under $100,000, presenting a structured business model that has already been tested in the market. For instance, some popular franchise opportunities include home-based travel agencies, pet care services, or small maintenance services (Stevens, 2022). Franchises come with the advantage of brand recognition and established operational procedures, reducing the learning curve for new business owners. Moreover, franchisors generally provide training and ongoing support, making it easier for newcomers to navigate the challenges of running a business.

Online Businesses have gained significant traction in recent years and offer numerous opportunities for acquisition within this budget. E-commerce stores, content creation platforms, and digital marketing agencies are examples of online businesses frequently available for under $100,000. These ventures are particularly appealing to tech-savvy individuals who enjoy leveraging the power of the internet to reach customers. The benefits of purchasing an online business include low overhead costs, flexibility in working hours, and the potential to operate from virtually anywhere in the world. Additionally, the scalability of online businesses is a significant advantage; with effective digital strategies, these businesses can quickly grow their customer base and revenue.

Local Brick-and-Mortar Stores also present viable options for aspiring entrepreneurs on a budget. Establishments like laundromats, small retail stores, and food trucks are frequently available within the $100,000 range. Local businesses offer the unique advantage of serving a tangible community need, which can foster a loyal customer base. Laundromats, for instance, are a staple in many neighborhoods and generate consistent revenue due to their essential nature. Similarly, small retail stores can cater to niche markets, while food trucks provide flexible and mobile dining experiences that have grown increasingly popular.

Purchasing a local brick-and-mortar store often includes acquiring existing equipment, inventory, and lease agreements, which can significantly reduce the time required to get the business up and running. It's important to evaluate the location and market demand carefully, as these factors will heavily influence the success of the venture.

Closing Remarks

This chapter has laid out the foundational benefits of purchasing an existing small business, especially one priced under $100,000. By exploring key advantages such as inheriting an established customer base, adopting a pre-existing operational framework, and leveraging brand recognition, we've demonstrated how these acquisitions can offer immediate stability and reduce initial risks. The potential for growth through innovative strategies also creates exciting opportunities for new owners to inject fresh perspectives and achieve greater success.

As you consider venturing into the world of business ownership, remember that buying an existing business provides a solid platform on which to build your entrepreneurial dreams. The insights provided in this chapter highlight why this path can be more secure and rewarding than starting from scratch. Whether you're drawn to service-based industries, franchises, online businesses, or local brick-and-mortar stores, the potential for success is vast.

Embrace these opportunities with optimism, and let the journey toward your business aspirations begin with confidence and clarity.

Chapter 3
Researching Viable Business Opportunities

Researching viable business opportunities involves the essential process of identifying and shortlisting suitable businesses to purchase for under $100,000. This chapter serves as a comprehensive guide to navigating this journey, providing practical strategies and insights to help aspiring entrepreneurs find lucrative business prospects within their budget. By focusing on accessible methods and resources, readers will gain confidence and clarity in their search for the perfect business opportunity.

Throughout this chapter, we will explore various avenues for discovering businesses for sale, starting with leveraging online marketplaces and tapping into personal networks. We will also delve into the invaluable role of business brokers, who can streamline the purchasing process with expert advice and connections. Direct outreach techniques will be discussed, highlighting how proactive efforts can uncover hidden opportunities. By examining these strategies and more, readers will be well-equipped to embark on their entrepreneurial venture with informed decisions and a clear path to success.

Where to find businesses for sale

Navigating the path to business ownership can be daunting, but knowing where to find viable opportunities is a critical first step. This section aims to provide readers with practical resources and platforms to discover available businesses that fit their budget, facilitating the journey toward realizing their entrepreneurial dreams. Let's explore some key strategies for uncovering small businesses available for purchase under $100,000.

One of the most accessible and effective ways to find businesses for sale is through online marketplaces. Websites like BizBuySell, BusinessBroker.net, and BizQuest specialize in small business listings, offering extensive catalogs of businesses across various industries. These platforms are particularly advantageous because they allow prospective buyers to filter search results based on specific criteria such as price, location, and industry. For instance, if you're looking for a bakery in a particular city within a set budget, these filters can narrow down the search, saving valuable time and effort. Additionally, setting up alerts for new listings ensures that buyers are notified as soon as relevant opportunities become available, enabling timely responses to attractive offers.

Networking also plays a crucial role in finding business opportunities. Leveraging personal and professional connections can often lead to discovering businesses that are not publicly listed for sale. Informal conversations with friends, colleagues, or acquaintances can reveal leads before they hit the market. For example, a casual chat at a social gathering might lead to learning about a local café owner considering retirement. Attending local business expos, trade shows, and community events can also be highly beneficial. These gatherings offer direct access to a network of business owners and sellers, presenting opportunities to connect face-to-face and discuss potential sales. Engaging with industry-specific forums or groups can further expand your reach, uncovering hidden opportunities in niche markets.

Business brokers are another invaluable resource in the business purchasing process. Brokers have the expertise and networks to provide insights into the buying process, making it smoother and more efficient. They can guide buyers through complex negotiations and paperwork, ensuring that all legal and financial aspects are correctly handled. It's essential to select a broker who specializes in small businesses under $100,000, as they will have a better understanding of the unique challenges and opportunities within this price range. While brokers may charge a fee for their services, the value they add often justifies the cost by streamlining the process and increasing the likelihood of finding a suitable business.

Direct approaches can also yield fruitful results when searching for businesses to buy. Reaching out directly to business owners demonstrates proactivity and can uncover opportunities not officially listed for sale. Crafting an effective outreach message is vital in this strategy. A well-written message should introduce yourself, express genuine interest in the business, and inquire about the owner's plans for the future. For example, "Hello, my name is Jane, and I am interested in purchasing a local bakery. I recently came across your lovely shop and wondered if you might be open to discussing potential sale opportunities." Such messages indicate sincerity and can initiate conversations that lead to buying opportunities.

Evaluating industry trends and market demand

Assessing the viability of business opportunities is a critical step for anyone looking to purchase a small business. To make informed purchasing decisions, it's essential to understand both current and projected market conditions. This subpoint aims to provide readers with practical tools and methods to evaluate these aspects, ensuring that the business you buy has the potential for success.

One key approach is utilizing market research tools. Tools like Google Trends are invaluable for assessing demand and understanding how interest in various industries changes over time. By entering relevant keywords, you can see the popularity of specific business ideas and identify seasonal trends. This insight helps you gauge whether a particular business opportunity aligns with consumer interests or if it risks being part of an oversaturated market. Additionally, industry reports from reputable sources offer comprehensive data on market size, growth rates, and competitive dynamics. These reports often highlight emerging trends and can reveal gaps in the market that a new business could exploit. Websites that track consumer behavior and spending patterns, such as Nielsen and Statista, also provide crucial information on what customers are currently buying and might purchase in the future.

Understanding market saturation is another important consideration. A thorough analysis can help you determine if there's room for another player in the field or if the market is already crowded. High competition can mean lower chances of success unless your business offers a unique value proposition. Conversely, less saturated markets might present more opportunities but require careful evaluation to ensure there's sufficient demand to support the business.

Industry growth analysis is another vital component in assessing business viability. Start by investigating historical trends to identify industries experiencing significant growth or decline. For example, publicly available data from government agencies or trade associations typically show long-term trends in different sectors. Look at graphs and reports that chart growth rates over several years to forecast future performance. The technology sector, for instance, has shown consistent growth, making it potentially favorable for investment. Conversely, industries in decline, like traditional retail stores, may pose higher risks. Understanding macroeconomic factors that impact specific industries is also crucial. Factors such as regulatory changes, technological advancements, or economic cycles can heavily influence industry dynamics. For instance, the renewable energy sector has grown due to increasing environmental regulations and consumer awareness, presenting lucrative opportunities for those interested in green technologies.

Next, target market assessment focuses on understanding who your customers are and how to reach them effectively. Knowing customer demographics such as age, gender, income level, and location helps tailor your business offerings to meet their needs. Conducting surveys or focus groups can provide direct feedback on your business ideas, revealing whether there's genuine interest among potential customers. These assessments can be done using tools like SurveyMonkey or Google Forms, which allow you to gather valuable insights quickly and efficiently. Demographic trends also play a significant role in business viability. For example, an aging population might increase demand for healthcare services, while younger demographics might drive growth in tech startups or eco-friendly products. Keeping an eye on these trends helps ensure that the business you plan to purchase aligns with future market needs.

Analyzing the competitive landscape is equally crucial in evaluating business opportunities. Conducting a SWOT analysis (Strengths, Weaknesses, Opportunities, Threats) provides a clear picture of where your business stands compared to competitors. Strengths and weaknesses are internal factors, such as your business's unique capabilities or areas needing improvement. Opportunities and threats are external factors, encompassing market conditions and competitive pressures. For example, a strength might be a proprietary product that fills a market gap, whereas a threat could be a well-established competitor with significant market share. Benchmarking key performance indicators (KPIs) such as sales revenue, profit margins, and customer retention rates against competitors can shed light on how well your business performs within the industry. It helps identify areas for improvement and strategies for gaining a competitive edge.

Understanding your competitors can also reveal unique selling propositions (USPs) or opportunities for differentiation. By analyzing what competitors offer and identifying their shortcomings, you can position your business to meet unmet customer needs. For instance, if competitors provide good quality but lack excellent customer service, emphasizing superior customer support could set your business apart. Likewise, innovation in product features, pricing strategies, or marketing approaches can create distinct advantages.

Bringing It All Together

Throughout this chapter, we delved into essential strategies for identifying and shortlisting suitable businesses to purchase for under $100,000. By leveraging online marketplaces, networking opportunities, business brokers, and direct approaches, you can uncover a wealth of viable options within your budget. These methods not only streamline the search process but also maximize your chances of finding the perfect business to meet your entrepreneurial aspirations.

In addition to these practical strategies, evaluating industry trends and market demand plays a pivotal role in making informed purchasing decisions. By utilizing market research tools and analyzing competitive landscapes, you ensure that the business you select is positioned for success. This comprehensive approach empowers you to navigate the business buying process with confidence and clarity, setting you on a path toward achieving your entrepreneurial goals.

Chapter 4
Assessing Financial Health

Assessing the financial health of a prospective business is a crucial step in making a sound investment decision. Investors need to be confident that their capital will be wisely placed, with minimal risk and maximum potential for return. Understanding the strengths and weaknesses of a company's financial position provides valuable insights into its viability. A thorough analysis of financial statements, such as balance sheets and income statements, lays the groundwork for assessing whether a business is financially stable or if it harbors hidden risks that could hinder future growth.

In this chapter, we delve into the essential steps necessary to evaluate financial viability thoroughly. We'll explore how reviewing financial statements can paint a clear picture of a company's assets, liabilities, and equity. We will discuss the significance of working capital and the importance of distinguishing between current and long-term liabilities. Additionally, we'll examine revenue streams, expense structures, and net profit margins to identify areas of strength and potential concern. By analyzing trends over multiple periods, we can uncover patterns that indicate growth or decline in profitability. Finally, we will highlight the importance of evaluating operational cash flows versus financing activities and review financial practices to spot any anomalies or irregularities. This structured approach ensures that investors are well-equipped to make informed decisions aligned with their goals.

Reviewing Financial Statements

To assess the financial health of a prospective business, a critical examination of its financial statements is essential. These statements provide a window into the company's performance and stability, offering invaluable insights into whether it is a sound investment. By carefully analyzing financial documents, investors can make informed decisions that align with their goals.

Let's start with the balance sheet, which offers a snapshot of a company's financial structure at a specific point in time. The balance sheet lists the company's assets, liabilities, and equity, giving us a clear picture of what the company owns and owes. Understanding this document helps identify the financial foundation upon which the company stands. For instance, a company with substantial assets relative to its liabilities may be considered financially stable, whereas one weighed down by debt could pose higher investment risk.

Recognizing the importance of working capital is also crucial as it indicates short-term financial health. Working capital, calculated by subtracting current liabilities from current assets, shows if the company has enough resources to cover its short-term obligations. A positive working capital suggests good liquidity, meaning the company can meet its immediate expenses and continue operations without financial strain.

Distinguishing between current and long-term liabilities aids in assessing risk. Current liabilities are debts due within a year, such as accounts payable or short-term loans, while long-term liabilities include obligations like mortgages or bonds payable over a longer period. A company with a high ratio of long-term liabilities to total liabilities might show a more stable financial footing, as its immediate debt pressure is lower.

Next, we delve into evaluating revenue streams and expense structures, which uncovers potential areas of concern or opportunity. By examining how a company generates income and manages its costs, investors can identify strengths and weaknesses in its business model. For example, a firm with diversified revenue streams may be better positioned to weather economic downturns, while heavy reliance on a single source of income could be risky.

Analyzing net profit margin gives insight into operational efficiency. This metric, calculated by dividing net income by total revenue, indicates how much profit a company makes for every dollar of revenue. A higher net profit margin suggests that the company operates efficiently, keeping costs low and maximizing earnings. Conversely, a lower margin may signal inefficiencies or high costs that could erode profitability over time.

Recognizing trends over multiple periods highlights growth or decline in profitability. By comparing financial data across several years, investors can spot patterns that reveal the company's trajectory. Consistent revenue growth and stable or improving profit margins typically signify a healthy, growing business. On the other hand, declining profits or erratic performance might raise red flags about the company's viability.

Determining operational cash flows versus financing activities reveals sustainability. Operational cash flow, derived from core business operations, indicates if the company generates sufficient cash to sustain itself. It's vital for companies to have robust operational cash flows, ensuring they can reinvest in the business, pay off debt, and cover day-to-day expenses. In contrast, cash flow from financing activities includes funds raised through loans or equity issues. Heavy reliance on such financing might suggest that a company is compensating for weak operational performance, raising concerns about long-term sustainability.

Reviewing a company's financial practices helps identify anomalies or irregularities. This involves looking beyond the numbers to understand accounting methods and policies. For instance, aggressive revenue recognition or unusual expense categorization could distort financial results, misleading investors. Ensuring transparency and adherence to standard accounting principles enhances trust in the financial statements' accuracy.

Understanding Key Financial Ratios

Understanding key financial ratios is essential for assessing the financial health of a prospective business. These ratios provide valuable insights into the company's performance, risk levels, and overall viability as an investment. By examining various financial ratios, potential investors can make more informed decisions and better understand the strengths and weaknesses of a business.

High liquidity ratios are one of the first indicators to consider. Liquidity ratios measure a company's ability to meet its short-term obligations using its most liquid assets. Common liquidity ratios include the current ratio and the quick ratio. The current ratio is calculated by dividing current assets by current liabilities. A high current ratio suggests that the company has sufficient resources to cover its short-term debts, which indicates good financial health. Similarly, the quick ratio, also known as the acid-test ratio, excludes inventory from current assets and compares the result to current liabilities. A high quick ratio further confirms that the company can easily meet its immediate financial obligations without relying on inventory sales. High liquidity ratios provide reassurance to investors that the business is not at risk of defaulting on short-term debts, making it a safer investment.

Another crucial financial ratio to consider is the return on investment (ROI). ROI measures the profitability of an investment relative to its cost, helping investors gauge the business's ability to generate returns. To calculate ROI, divide the net profit by the total investment cost and multiply by 100 to express it as a percentage. A high ROI indicates that the business efficiently uses its invested capital to generate profits, making it an attractive investment opportunity. For instance, if a company invested $100,000 in new machinery and generated $150,000 in additional revenue, the ROI would be 50%. Understanding ROI allows investors to compare different investment opportunities and choose those with the highest potential for returns. It also helps investors identify businesses that consistently deliver strong financial performance, enhancing their confidence in the long-term sustainability of the investment.

Leverage ratios are equally important when assessing a company's financial health. These ratios measure the extent to which a business is financed through debt compared to equity. High leverage ratios can signal a riskier investment due to increased debt obligations. One common leverage ratio is the debt-to-equity ratio, which is calculated by dividing total debt by shareholders' equity. A high debt-to-equity ratio indicates that the company relies heavily on borrowed funds, which could lead to financial instability if it cannot meet its debt repayments. Another leverage ratio to consider is the interest coverage ratio, which measures a company's ability to pay interest on its outstanding debt. This ratio is calculated by dividing earnings before interest and taxes (EBIT) by interest expenses. A low interest coverage ratio suggests that the company may struggle to meet its interest payments, increasing the risk of default. By examining leverage ratios, investors can assess the level of financial risk associated with the business and determine whether it has a healthy balance between debt and equity financing.

Turnover rates are another vital aspect of financial analysis. Turnover rates indicate the effectiveness of a company's management in utilizing its resources to generate sales. High turnover rates suggest efficient management and effective use of assets, which contribute to overall business success. Two key turnover ratios to consider are the inventory turnover ratio and the accounts receivable turnover ratio. The inventory turnover ratio is calculated by dividing the cost of goods sold by average inventory. A high inventory turnover ratio indicates that the company quickly sells and replenishes its inventory, reducing the risk of obsolete stock and improving cash flow. On the other hand, the accounts receivable turnover ratio measures how effectively the company collects payments from customers. It is calculated by dividing net credit sales by average accounts receivable. A high accounts receivable turnover ratio suggests that the company promptly collects outstanding debts, improving liquidity and reducing the risk of bad debt. High turnover rates demonstrate that the company has robust operational efficiency and sound financial management practices, making it an appealing investment opportunity.

Concluding Thoughts

Analyzing the financial viability of a prospective business is a vital step in ensuring that your investment will align with your goals and provide sound returns. Through careful examination of financial statements, such as the balance sheet, income statement, and cash flow statement, you gain insights into the company's assets, liabilities, revenue streams, and expense structures. Understanding these documents helps identify whether a company is financially stable, operationally efficient, and capable of sustaining itself in the long term. Evaluating key financial ratios like liquidity, ROI, and leverage further allows you to gauge the overall health and risk levels associated with the business. These steps collectively offer a comprehensive view of the business's financial standing.

By recognizing trends, assessing working capital, and distinguishing between different types of liabilities, you can pinpoint growth opportunities or potential red flags. Financial ratios and turnover rates provide crucial indicators of how well the company utilizes its resources and manages debt. This thorough analysis equips you with the knowledge needed to make informed decisions, ensuring that your investment not only meets your current financial objectives but also holds promise for future growth. With these tools at your disposal, you are well-prepared to navigate the complexities of the business buying process and invest with confidence.

Chapter 5
Due Diligence

Conducting thorough due diligence is essential for a successful business acquisition. This process serves as your safeguard against unforeseen challenges and potential liabilities that could jeopardize your investment. By delving into the company's legal framework, you'll uncover the complexities of its structure, taxation obligations, and regulatory compliance. It is critical to understand the specifics of the entity you are acquiring, from Limited Liability Companies (LLCs) to corporations, partnerships, or sole proprietorships. Engaging legal experts in this preliminary stage can provide invaluable insights, ensuring clarity on both advantages and potential pitfalls. This foundational knowledge empowers you to make informed decisions and strategic adjustments post-acquisition.

Additionally, assessing the operational strengths and weaknesses of the target company is crucial. This involves a comprehensive review of key performance indicators (KPIs), operational processes, employee competence, and customer base analysis. Evaluating KPIs such as sales trends, customer retention rates, and operational efficiency offers a clear picture of the business's health. Scrutinizing day-to-day operations, from workflows to supply chain logistics, helps identify bottlenecks and areas for improvement. Employee evaluations reveal skill gaps and morale status, while understanding customer demographics and satisfaction levels informs future marketing and retention strategies. Together, these steps form a holistic approach to due diligence, maximizing the value and minimizing risks in your business acquisition journey.

Legal Considerations and Contracts

When considering an acquisition, one of the most critical steps is understanding the business structure of the company you are looking to buy. The type of entity—whether it's a Limited Liability Company (LLC), corporation, partnership, or sole proprietorship—can significantly impact your liabilities and tax obligations. For instance, an LLC typically offers limited liability protection, meaning that your personal assets are generally protected from business debts. On the other hand, corporations may offer different benefits, such as the ability to attract investors through stock issuance but come with their own set of regulatory requirements and potential double taxation issues.

To safeguard your investment, take time to thoroughly understand the business's legal framework. Engaging a legal expert specializing in business law can provide invaluable insights into the specific advantages and disadvantages each business structure offers. This step ensures you comprehend fully what you're getting into and arms you with the necessary knowledge to make adjustments post-acquisition if needed.

Equally important is reviewing existing contractual obligations the business holds. Contracts with suppliers, customers, and employees could contain hidden liabilities that can surface after you've taken ownership. Supplier contracts might have minimum purchase requirements or exclusivity clauses that limit your operational flexibility. Customer contracts could include service level agreements (SLAs) that necessitate high standards of performance, which could be challenging to maintain during the transition period. Employee agreements may have clauses related to severance, non-compete agreements, or ongoing benefits that could pose unexpected financial burdens.

To effectively navigate these complexities, it's advisable to carry out a comprehensive audit of all significant contracts. Pay special attention to terms that might not be immediately obvious but could impose considerable financial or operational constraints. Understanding these details upfront allows you to negotiate better terms or prepare adequately for potential challenges.

Another critical area requiring due diligence is the status of licenses and permits the business holds. Regulatory compliance is non-negotiable, and failure to maintain current and transferable licenses can lead to substantial legal penalties and operational disruptions. Verify that all municipal, state, and federal licenses are up-to-date and assess whether they will seamlessly transfer to you upon acquisition. Industries such as healthcare, food services, and manufacturing often have stringent licensing requirements, making this review vital for ensuring uninterrupted operations.

In addition to verifying the existence and currency of licenses, assess the process required to transfer them. Some licenses might need immediate renewal, or worse, new applications altogether under your ownership, which can be time-consuming and complicated. Proactively determining these factors can help anticipate and mitigate risks, thereby avoiding any compliance gaps that could adversely affect your business post-acquisition.

An often-overlooked aspect of due diligence revolves around contingencies and exit clauses embedded within the purchasing contract. These clauses serve as safety nets that protect your interests should unforeseen circumstances arise. For example, a contingency clause might stipulate that the acquisition is subject to the business passing a final inspection or certain financial thresholds being met. Exit clauses allow either party to terminate the contract under specified conditions without severe penalties.

A clear understanding of these clauses enables you to plan strategically and act decisively if things don't go as planned. They offer a way out or modifications to the deal terms, shielding you from making irrevocable commitments that turn out unfavorable. Your legal advisor can play a crucial role here by ensuring that all contingencies and exit options are explicitly defined and favorable to you as the buyer.

Given these multifaceted considerations, setting up a structured due diligence checklist tailored to the specific business you're acquiring is indispensable. Such a checklist would typically cover the following:

1. **Business Structure:** Identify the type of business entity and its respective legal and tax implications.

2. **Contractual Obligations:** Conduct a thorough review of existing contracts with suppliers, customers, and employees to identify any hidden liabilities.

3. **Licenses and Permits:** Verify all necessary licenses and permits are current and assess the process for their transfer post-acquisition.

4. **Contingencies and Exit Clauses:** Ensure that all contingencies and exit clauses in the purchasing contract are clearly understood and favorable to you.

Evaluating Operational Strengths and Weaknesses

Assessing the operational aspects of a business is crucial in identifying potential opportunities and threats that may influence a buyer's decision-making process. A thorough evaluation can provide insightful data to ensure that the acquisition aligns with strategic goals, minimizes risks, and maximizes value. This assessment involves several key components, beginning with Understanding Key Performance Indicators (KPIs).

Assessing Key Performance Indicators (KPIs)

KPIs are essential metrics that give an overview of a company's health and performance. These indicators can be segmented into different categories, such as sales, customer retention, and operational efficiency. Evaluating sales KPIs involves looking at revenue trends, growth rates, and market share. For instance, steady year-over-year revenue growth could indicate a strong product-market fit, whereas declining sales might signal underlying issues.

Customer retention is another critical KPI. High retention rates typically suggest customer satisfaction and loyalty, which are vital for sustained profitability. Conversely, low retention rates may point to problems with the product or service, competitive pressures, or poor customer relations.

Operational efficiency KPIs measure how well a company uses its resources to generate output. Metrics like inventory turnover, production cycle time, and cost per unit produced can highlight areas for improvement. An efficient operation is usually more profitable and resilient to market fluctuations.

When assessing KPIs, it's beneficial to benchmark them against industry standards. This comparison provides context and highlights where the business stands relative to its peers, thus identifying both strengths and weaknesses.

Operational Processes Review

Analyzing day-to-day operational processes reveals how effectively a business runs on a granular level. Operational reviews include scrutinizing workflows, supply chain logistics, and production methodologies. The goal is to identify bottlenecks that could hinder productivity and opportunities to enhance profitability.

Take, for example, a manufacturing business. Reviewing its production line might uncover inefficiencies such as outdated machinery or suboptimal workflow designs causing delays. Addressing these issues could involve investing in new technology, retraining staff, or redesigning the workspace for better flow.

In addition to physical processes, digital operations should also be examined. Assessing the use of software and technology can reveal how digital tools support—or hinder—efficiency. Automating routine tasks through software solutions can free up valuable human resources for more critical functions.

Implementing process improvements not only reduces costs but can also improve product quality and customer satisfaction. Efficient operations lead to shorter lead times, quicker delivery, and the ability to scale up production in response to demand spikes.

Staff Competence and Culture

Employees are the lifeblood of any organization, making it essential to evaluate their skills, morale, and the overall company culture. A competent, motivated workforce is more likely to embrace change and contribute positively to the transition post-acquisition.

Begin by assessing staff competence through performance reviews, skill assessments, and interviews. Identify key employees and understand their roles within the organization. Are there skill gaps that need addressing? Does the current workforce have the capacity to support future growth?

Morale is equally important. Employee satisfaction surveys, turnover rates, and informal conversations can offer insights into the workplace atmosphere. High morale indicates a positive work environment, whereas low morale might suggest underlying issues that need attention.

Company culture plays a significant role in employee performance and retention. Determine whether the existing culture aligns with your values and operational style. A cultural mismatch can lead to friction and disengagement among employees. If the cultures differ significantly, consider strategies for blending them post-acquisition to ensure a smooth integration.

Lastly, prepare for resource allocation by identifying training needs and developing integration plans. Equipping employees with necessary skills and aligning the team with new objectives ensures a smoother transition and faster achievement of post-acquisition goals.

Customer Base Analysis

Understanding the business's customer demographics and satisfaction levels is pivotal in shaping post-acquisition marketing and retention strategies. Analyzing customer data includes examining demographic information, purchasing behaviors, and feedback from satisfaction surveys.

Demographic analysis helps in identifying target markets and tailoring products or services to meet specific needs. For example, if the majority of customers are millennials, marketing efforts can be focused on social media campaigns and digital engagement strategies.

Purchasing behavior insights allow you to refine product offerings and pricing strategies. Frequent purchase patterns indicate high demand items, while stagnant stock might need reevaluation or discontinuation. Additionally, identifying any seasonal trends can help in planning inventory and marketing campaigns more effectively.

Customer satisfaction surveys shed light on how clients perceive products and services. High satisfaction levels typically translate into customer loyalty and positive word-of-mouth. On the other hand, negative feedback requires prompt action to address concerns and improve the overall customer experience.

Tailoring marketing strategies post-acquisition involves leveraging these insights to create targeted campaigns aimed at retaining existing customers and attracting new ones. This might include personalized promotions, loyalty programs, and enhanced customer service initiatives. Effective retention strategies ensure that the acquired customer base remains loyal and engaged during and after the transition period.

Summary and Reflections

Conducting thorough due diligence is vital to navigating the complexities of business acquisitions. This chapter has outlined the importance of legal considerations, from understanding the business structure to meticulously reviewing contracts with suppliers, customers, and employees. By ensuring all licenses and permits are up-to-date and transferable, you can avoid legal penalties and operational disruptions. Equally crucial is the comprehension of contingencies and exit clauses within the purchasing contract, offering a strategic safety net should unforeseen circumstances arise.

On the operational front, evaluating key performance indicators, scrutinizing daily processes, and assessing staff competence provide valuable insights into the strengths and weaknesses of the business. Analyzing the customer base helps shape effective post-acquisition marketing and retention strategies. Through diligent examination of these areas, you can ensure that the acquisition aligns with your strategic goals, minimizes risks, and maximizes value. A structured approach to due diligence equips you with the knowledge needed to make informed decisions and secure a successful transition.

Chapter 6
Valuing a Business

Valuing a business is essential to ensuring you make informed financial decisions and negotiate effectively. When considering the purchase of a business priced under $100,000, understanding its true worth can be both enlightening and empowering. This chapter will explore various methods that can help potential buyers get a clearer picture of what they are investing in, providing insights into different aspects of business valuation.

To assist you in this journey, we will delve into multiple techniques for evaluating a business. The Market Comparison Approach will show how comparing similar businesses can set realistic price expectations. We'll also examine the Asset-Based Valuation method, which assesses the value of tangible and intangible assets, and the Income Approach, which focuses on future earnings. Additionally, the Discounted Cash Flow Analysis will provide a comprehensive view by estimating future cash flows in present terms. These methodologies will collectively equip you with a robust strategy to determine the right price to pay, laying the foundation for successful negotiations and long-term business success.

Methods of Business Valuation

Determining the value of a business can be a complex task, especially when it comes to determining the appropriate price for a business under $100,000. Various techniques can assist potential buyers in gaining a clearer understanding of the true worth of the business they are considering. These methods not only provide concrete figures but also offer insights into the strengths and weaknesses of the enterprise.

To begin with, one of the most straightforward techniques is the Market Comparison Approach. This method involves examining how similar businesses are valued in the market. By using comparable sales data, potential buyers can establish a benchmark that reflects what buyers are willing to pay. For example, if a coffee shop in a similar location with comparable revenue streams recently sold for $90,000, this provides a tangible reference point. This approach helps anchor expectations and ensures buyers do not overpay. Additionally, looking at multiple similar businesses allows for a more rounded perspective, minimizing the risk of skewed data from outliers.

Another valuable technique is Asset-Based Valuation, which focuses on assessing the value of the company's tangible and intangible assets. Tangible assets include things like equipment, inventory, and property, while intangible assets might encompass trademarks, brand reputation, and customer lists. The key here is to take stock of everything the business owns and to assign a monetary value to these assets. For instance, if a printing business has state-of-the-art equipment valued at $50,000 and a coveted client list, these elements play a crucial role in determining its overall worth. This method is particularly useful for businesses that may not have high revenue but possess significant physical or intellectual properties.

The Income Approach is another powerful valuation method, emphasizing the future earnings potential of the business. This technique evaluates a business based on its expected future profits, guiding buyers towards opportunities that promise profitable returns. To apply this method, one would review the historical financial performance of the business, projecting future revenues and expenses to estimate potential profitability. For example, if a bakery has shown consistent profit growth of 5% per year, this trend can be extended to forecast future income. The Income Approach places considerable importance on the sustainability of profits, making it a preferred choice for those prioritizing steady income streams.

Furthermore, the Discounted Cash Flow (DCF) Analysis offers a detailed view by estimating future cash flows and discounting them to their present value. This method requires a projection of the business's cash flows over a certain period, adjusted for the time value of money. Essentially, money today is worth more than the same amount in the future due to its potential earning capacity. For instance, a small retail store might generate projected cash flows of $20,000 annually over the next five years. By applying a discount rate reflecting the risk factor and opportunity cost, these future cash flows are translated into today's value. The DCF analysis is particularly insightful as it accounts for both the magnitude and timing of expected cash flows, providing a comprehensive evaluation of future financial performance.

Each of these techniques brings unique insights and advantages. Using the Market Comparison Approach, buyers gain a real-world context by benchmarking against actual market transactions. This can prevent emotional decision-making and provide reassurance about the price being paid. The Asset-Based Valuation grounds the assessment in concrete, identifiable items, making it easier to justify expenditures based on existing resources. Meanwhile, the Income Approach emphasizes long-term profitability, steering buyers toward investments poised for sustained success. Lastly, the DCF Analysis presents a forward-looking perspective that values the anticipated cash flows' present worth, offering a nuanced understanding of future benefits.

It's important to note that no single valuation method is definitively superior; rather, a combination of approaches often yields the most accurate and reliable results. Combining these insights fosters a robust valuation strategy, helping buyers navigate various scenarios and financial landscapes. For instance, while the Market Comparison Approach might suggest a fair market price, integrating the Asset-Based Valuation could reveal undervalued assets that enhance the business's attractiveness.

Understanding these techniques and applying them diligently equips prospective buyers with the knowledge and confidence needed for effective negotiations. Armed with solid valuation methods, buyers can better articulate their reasons for offering a specific price, ensuring that their financial decisions are well-founded and strategically sound. This comprehensive understanding not only facilitates a successful purchase but also lays the groundwork for future business prosperity.

Negotiation Strategies for Final Pricing

Navigating the intricate landscape of buying a business without overspending requires a strategic approach to negotiations. With the ultimate goal of securing the best deal for a business under $100,000, it's essential to arm yourself with effective negotiation tactics. Let's explore how preparation, establishing an anchor point, showing value, and maintaining flexibility can lead you toward a successful purchase.

Preparation and Research

Preparation is the cornerstone of any successful negotiation. Before stepping into negotiations, invest time in researching the business thoroughly. Understanding its financial health, market position, competitive landscape, and growth potential builds a robust foundation for your bargaining strategy. Look at recent financial statements, analyze key performance indicators, and consider speaking with industry experts. Not only does this knowledge empower you, but it also builds confidence. When you're well-informed, you can articulate a compelling rationale for why your offer makes sense.

For example, if you're eyeing a small café, delve into its monthly revenue trends, profit margins, and customer base. Know how it compares with similar cafés in the area. Armed with such information, you can confidently discuss specifics with the seller, showcasing your preparedness and seriousness in making a fair deal. Your research will serve as a shield against overpaying and provide clear grounds for your offer.

Establishing an Anchor Point

Negotiation 101: always start with a lower offer than what you're ultimately willing to pay. This tactic, known as establishing an anchor point, sets the stage for bargaining within your desired price range. Calculate a reasonable starting bid by assessing the valuation findings and keeping your maximum budget in mind.

Let's say you've valued the business at $80,000, considering factors like assets, revenue, and market conditions. An opening offer of $70,000 gives you room to maneuver while signaling to the seller that you're serious but looking for the best possible deal. It's essential to back up your initial offer with concrete reasons derived from your research. The goal here is not to offend but to engage the seller in a dialogue where both parties can work towards a mutually beneficial agreement.

Showing Value

When a seller presents their asking price, it's imperative to demonstrate why you believe a lower price is justified. Present counterarguments based on your valuation findings to underscore your offer. Highlight aspects such as outdated equipment, declining revenue, or upcoming expenses that may have been overlooked. By doing so, you encourage sellers to view their offering through a more critical lens.

Imagine negotiating the purchase of a tech startup. You might point out that although the business has immense potential, it requires significant investment in updating software or marketing to achieve that potential. Such constructive feedback helps balance expectations and paves the way for a discussion grounded in reality. Showing value isn't merely about pointing out flaws; it's about guiding the seller to a more accurate valuation of their business.

Flexibility and Compromise

Negotiations are not always about sticking rigidly to a set price. Demonstrating flexibility and willingness to compromise positions you as a serious and approachable buyer. Consider negotiating terms beyond just the price, such as payment schedules, inclusion of assets, or transitional support periods. These elements can be pivotal in closing a deal that's favorable for both parties.

For instance, you might agree to the seller's asking price if they provide a six-month training period post-sale. This ensures a smooth transition and immediate operational continuity, which could be invaluable for sustaining the business. Alternatively, negotiating a staggered payment plan can ease financial strain, making the deal more attractive to both the buyer and the seller.

Balancing flexibility and firmness is key. While you remain open to compromises on certain elements, ensure these adjustments do not undermine your primary goals. Being adaptable showcases your commitment to finding common ground, fostering trust, and building a positive rapport with the seller.

Insights and Implications

In this chapter, we've explored several key methods to determine the right price for a business under $100,000. By understanding and applying techniques like the Market Comparison Approach, Asset-Based Valuation, Income Approach, and Discounted Cash Flow Analysis, buyers gain essential insights into the true worth of a business. These valuation techniques help prospective buyers make informed decisions, ensuring they do not overpay and that they recognize the strengths and weaknesses inherent in each business opportunity.

Equipped with these valuation methods, prospective buyers can approach negotiations with confidence and clarity. Knowing how to prepare, establish an anchor point, show value, and maintain flexibility during negotiations ensures a strategic and effective bargaining process. This comprehensive knowledge enables buyers to justify their offers convincingly, navigate financial discussions smoothly, and secure favorable deals. Ultimately, mastering these strategies paves the way for making well-founded financial decisions and achieving business success.

Chapter 7
Securing Financing

Securing financing is crucial for acquiring a small business, and it involves choosing the right funding method. With a variety of traditional and alternative financing options available, understanding their unique benefits and challenges is essential for making an informed decision. Both types have their pros and cons, and finding the right fit can significantly impact the success of your business acquisition.

In this chapter, you'll explore both traditional methods like bank loans and credit unions alongside alternative solutions such as crowdfunding, peer-to-peer lending, and microloans. You'll also delve into the practical steps for applying for these types of financing, including what lenders typically require. Real-world examples and case studies will illustrate different financing strategies, providing valuable insights to help you navigate the complexities of securing the necessary funds to buy a business under $100,000.

Traditional vs. Alternative Financing

Securing financing for small business acquisitions requires a clear understanding of both traditional and alternative financing methods. This section will clarify the distinctions between these two types, providing readers with a spectrum of options suitable for their budget constraints.

Traditional financing methods have long been the cornerstone for business transactions. Conventional funding sources like bank loans and credit unions offer tried-and-true avenues for securing capital. Banks are known to provide lower interest rates compared to other financing methods, which can result in significant savings over time. Additionally, credit unions often extend favorable terms to their members, making them an attractive option for borrowing funds. However, securing a loan from these traditional institutions involves meeting rigorous criteria.

Understanding the application process for traditional loans is crucial. Banks typically require a comprehensive business plan, detailed financial statements, and evidence of a solid credit history. Potential borrowers must also be prepared to demonstrate their ability to repay the loan through cash flow projections and past performance metrics. Furthermore, lenders usually expect collateral as security for the loan, which could include personal assets or business property. By preparing thoroughly and presenting a strong financial profile, applicants can increase their chances of approval.

For those who might find the stringent requirements of traditional loans challenging, alternative financing methods offer viable options. Crowdfunding, peer-to-peer lending, and microloans are gaining popularity due to their accessibility and flexibility. Crowdfunding platforms, such as Kickstarter and Indiegogo, allow entrepreneurs to raise small amounts of money from a large number of people, bypassing the need for a formal loan application. Peer-to-peer lending websites like LendingClub connect borrowers directly with individual investors, often leading to faster approval times than conventional banks. Microloans, offered by organizations like the Small Business Administration (SBA), provide smaller loan amounts that are easier to qualify for, particularly for businesses that do not have an extensive credit history.

While alternative financing options offer speed and ease of access, they come with potential drawbacks that must be considered. One significant disadvantage is the higher interest rates typically associated with these non-conventional funding sources. Crowdfunding campaigns may also require considerable effort to market effectively, ensuring enough backers contribute to reach the financial goal.

Peer-to-peer lending agreements can include less favorable terms than traditional bank loans, emphasizing the importance of reading all fine print before committing.

When comparing the pros and cons of each financing method, it is essential to consider various factors. Traditional financing methods offer stability, lower interest rates, and structured repayment schedules. The predictability of these loans helps businesses manage cash flow more effectively. Conversely, alternative financing provides quick access to funds, which can be critical for seizing immediate business opportunities. However, the higher costs associated with these methods may strain financial resources over time. Practical experiences and anecdotes from other business owners reveal that while some entrepreneurs find success with crowdfunding, others benefit from the credibility and support offered by traditional lenders.

Evaluating terms and repayment schedules is vital in assessing how different financing options impact cash flow. Bank loans generally come with fixed interest rates and monthly payments that make budgeting straightforward. In contrast, repayment schedules for alternative financing options can vary widely, sometimes requiring more frequent payments or fluctuating interest rates. Understanding these dynamics will help readers foresee any potential cash flow challenges and adapt their financial planning accordingly.

Choosing the right financing ultimately depends on individual circumstances. Evaluating personal situations involves assessing current financial health, existing debt levels, and future business goals. Aligning financing choices with business objectives ensures that the selected method supports long-term growth rather than creating undue financial stress. Consulting with financial advisors can provide valuable insights into navigating the complexities of different financing options, helping to tailor decisions to specific needs.

One practical guideline when choosing the appropriate financing option is to adjust personal budgets to accommodate new financial obligations. For instance, if selecting a traditional bank loan with fixed monthly payments, it's wise to ensure there's sufficient monthly income to cover these expenses without compromising other operational costs. On the other hand, if opting for a more flexible alternative financing route, carefully monitoring income and expenses will prevent unexpected shortfalls. Engaging in diligent budget adjustments early on prepares business owners for sustainable financial management.

Leveraging Seller Financing Opportunities

Seller financing is a powerful option for small business acquisition that can significantly ease the financial burden on buyers. This subpoint will introduce seller financing, discuss its benefits, and provide practical tips on negotiating and securing such arrangements. Additionally, real-world case studies will be explored to illustrate its effectiveness.

What is Seller Financing?

Seller financing, also known as owner financing, refers to a transaction where the seller provides a loan to the buyer to facilitate the purchase of the business. Here, instead of seeking external funding from banks or financial institutions, the buyer makes installment payments directly to the seller. This arrangement bypasses the stringent qualification criteria typically associated with traditional loans, making it more accessible for many buyers.

One of the key benefits of seller financing is the flexibility it offers. For buyers, it can mean lower upfront costs, reduced dependency on external credit sources, and faster transaction closures. Sellers, on the other hand, often benefit through higher selling prices and steady income in the form of interest payments. Both parties are spared the complex bureaucracy of conventional financing, which can streamline negotiations and foster mutual trust.

Negotiating Seller Financing Terms

Effective negotiation is crucial for securing favorable seller financing terms. Building rapport with the seller is the first step, as establishing a good relationship can lead to more amicable discussions. Buyers should take time to understand the seller's motivations and concerns, which may range from financial security to ensuring the business continues to thrive under new ownership.

When proposing payment terms, it's essential to strike a balance that protects both parties' interests. Reasonable payment schedules that demonstrate your commitment and ability to uphold the agreement can instill confidence in the seller. Consider suggesting regular payments over a period that aligns with your cash flow projections while including a fair interest rate that compensates the seller adequately.

Examples of favorable terms might include starting with a smaller down payment, followed by incremental monthly installments over several years. Balloon payments, which involve paying a larger sum at the end of the term, can also be appealing if they align with anticipated revenue growth or planned refinancing options. By clearly outlining your proposal and showcasing your financial diligence, you can create a compelling case for why the seller should consider your offer.

Securing Seller Financing

Once an agreement is reached, the process of securing seller financing begins. One of the critical components is drafting a well-structured promissory note, which serves as a legal document outlining the terms of the loan. This note should specify the loan amount, interest rate, repayment schedule, and any collateral involved. It is beneficial to consult with legal professionals to ensure all aspects are covered, preventing potential disputes later on.

Interest rates in seller financing can vary widely but typically fall between the rates offered by traditional banks and those of higher-risk loans. It's important to negotiate a rate that reflects the risk level while remaining fair to both parties. Repayment schedules should be realistic and align with projected business revenues to avoid straining the operation's cash flow.

Buyers must also be aware of potential pitfalls in seller financing. One significant risk is the possibility of defaulting on payments, which could result in losing the business and any equity built up. Thoroughly assessing your financial capacity and ensuring that conservative projections support your payment plan can mitigate this risk.

Case Studies of Success

Real-world examples can provide invaluable insights into the mechanics and benefits of seller financing. Take, for instance, a scenario involving a small bakery purchase. The buyer, with limited access to traditional financing, negotiated a seller-financed deal with ten percent down and monthly payments over five years. This arrangement allowed the buyer to retain working capital for operational needs, while the seller received steady income and retained a vested interest in the business's continued success.

Another example could be a landscaping company where the buyer and seller agreed on a balloon payment structure. With seasonal fluctuations in revenue, this approach provided the buyer with manageable monthly payments during off-peak months, culminating in a larger payoff during high-revenue periods. The seller benefited from a consistent income stream and a substantial final payment, aligning with their retirement plans.

These case studies highlight lessons learned, such as the importance of detailed financial planning and open communication between parties. They also emphasize the versatility of seller financing across different industries, demonstrating its application beyond specific business types.

Final Insights

In this chapter, we've explored a variety of financing options tailored to small business acquisitions under $100,000. From traditional bank loans and credit union offerings to innovative alternatives like crowdfunding and peer-to-peer lending, each method comes with its own set of advantages and challenges. By understanding these options, potential buyers can make informed decisions that align with their financial goals and business aspirations.

Choosing the right financing option is crucial for the smooth transition and future success of any small business acquisition. Armed with knowledge about the different financing methods, readers can now confidently evaluate their personal circumstances, adjust budgets accordingly, and seek professional advice when necessary. This thoughtful approach will ensure sustainable financial management and support long-term growth, empowering entrepreneurs to achieve their dreams of business ownership.

Chapter 8
Closing the Deal

Closing a deal is an intricate process that requires meticulous preparation and strategic planning. This chapter dives into the final steps necessary to successfully purchase a business, emphasizing the importance of being thorough with every detail. As buyers approach the closing stage, it becomes imperative to handle essential documents correctly and ensure each party's interests are safeguarded. The efforts invested in these final stages can set the tone for a successful transition and establish a strong foundation for future operations.

Readers will find comprehensive guidance on preparing key documents like the Letter of Intent, Purchase Agreement, and Closing Statement. Each document plays a critical role in documenting the terms of the sale, outlining obligations, and detailing financials to avoid any surprises later on. Additionally, the chapter highlights the significance of Transfer Documents, which legally facilitate the handover of ownership. By understanding and managing each document effectively, buyers can minimize risks and pave the way for a smooth transition. The chapter further explores strategies for managing the post-acquisition phase, ensuring continuity and stability in business operations. Through practical advice and detailed examples, readers will gain the confidence needed to navigate the complexities of closing a business deal and executing a seamless ownership transition.

Preparing Closing Documents

Understanding the necessary documents for closing a business purchase is crucial for any prospective buyer. This subpoint aims to provide clarity on these essential documents and ensure that all legal requirements are met before finalizing the transaction.

First, let's discuss the Letter of Intent (LOI). It's an initial document that outlines the buyer's interest in purchasing the business and proposes the basic terms of the deal. Think of it as setting the stage for serious negotiations. The LOI doesn't bind the parties to go through with the deal but indicates the buyer's commitment and the general terms under which they are prepared to proceed. This document plays a crucial role in establishing expectations and signaling seriousness from both sides. Including details such as the purchase price, payment terms, and timelines can prevent misunderstandings later on. A well-crafted LOI serves as a roadmap for the subsequent stages of the acquisition process.

Next, we have the Purchase Agreement, the cornerstone of any business acquisition. Unlike the LOI, this document is legally binding and details every aspect of the sale. It minimizes ambiguities and protects the interests of both the buyer and the seller. The Purchase Agreement includes detailed descriptions of the assets being sold, liabilities being assumed, and specific terms like warranties, representations, and indemnities. For instance, if there are conditions about the maintenance of certain levels of working capital, those should be explicitly stated. Such details ensure that both parties are completely aware of their obligations and reduce the risk of disputes after the deal is closed. Crafting a thorough Purchase Agreement involves meticulous attention to detail and often requires professional legal assistance to ensure completeness and accuracy.

The Closing Statement is another critical document that cannot be overlooked. This statement provides a comprehensive summary of all financial aspects of the transaction. It lists out fees, expenses, adjustments, and the final purchase price. Transparency is paramount here, as it ensures both parties understand the financial implications of the deal. Imagine it as the receipt you receive after making a large purchase; it breaks down where every dollar is going. Detailed line items help avoid any hidden fees or unexpected costs that might arise post-closing. It's essential for the buyer to scrutinize this document closely to verify all calculations and adjustments. Any discrepancies found at this stage should be addressed immediately to prevent future conflicts.

Lastly, let's cover Transfer Documents. These facilitate the legal transfer of assets and liabilities from the seller to the buyer. This category includes deeds, titles, and necessary seller disclosures. Transfer Documents are pivotal in ensuring that everything agreed upon in the Purchase Agreement is officially transferred to the new owner. For example, if the business includes real estate, a property deed must be transferred. Similarly, intellectual property rights, licenses, and permits need proper documentation to confirm their transfer. Ensuring the completeness and correctness of these documents is vital because any oversight can lead to complications in asserting ownership later on. Seller disclosures play a significant role here; they ensure that the buyer is fully informed about any issues or liabilities associated with the assets being transferred.

A clear understanding and proper handling of these documents are paramount. Each document serves a distinct purpose and, together, they form the backbone of a seamless business acquisition process. They not only safeguard the interests of both parties but also pave the way for a smooth transition of ownership. Therefore, taking the time to understand each document, seeking professional advice, and ensuring all legal requirements are met will significantly contribute to a successful and stress-free closing of the deal.

Managing the Transition Effectively

Overseeing the transition phase post-acquisition is critical to ensuring continuity and stability in operations. Developing a comprehensive communication plan is essential in this regard. Clear, transparent communication helps minimize anxiety among employees and builds trust with clients. When employees understand their roles and the company's direction, they are more likely to remain engaged and productive. Likewise, clients feel reassured when they know the business they rely on will continue to meet their needs without disruption.

A robust communication plan includes regular updates about the transition's progress, addressing any concerns promptly and honestly. Holding meetings, sending out newsletters, and creating an accessible information hub can help disseminate information effectively. For instance, weekly team meetings can offer a platform for discussing ongoing changes and future plans. This allows employees to voice their concerns and leaders to provide clarity. Similarly, personalized emails to key clients explaining how the transition will impact them and what measures are in place to ensure seamless service can foster confidence.

Engaging with existing staff and customers is another crucial strategy. Retaining the institutional knowledge of current employees is vital for maintaining operational continuity. These individuals are familiar with the daily workings of the business and have established relationships with clients. Regular one-on-one meetings with key staff members can help reassure them of their value to the new ownership and maintain morale. This engagement should extend beyond formal interactions—casual conversations and inclusive activities can also help build rapport and ease the transition.

For customers, personal engagement can make a significant difference. Hosting meet-and-greet events where clients can interact with the new owners is a valuable way to build trust and show commitment. Additionally, personalized communications such as thank-you notes or follow-up calls after the acquisition can reinforce the message that their business is valued and will continue to be a priority.

Assessing current operations and understanding any immediate needs is another important step. Conducting thorough due diligence during the acquisition process often reveals areas needing improvement or realignment with the buyer's vision. A comprehensive operational review post-acquisition helps identify these areas and develop strategies to address them. This can include evaluating workflows, technology systems, and organizational structures to ensure they support the overall business goals.

For example, if the acquired business relies on outdated software systems, investing in upgrades could enhance efficiency and align operations with the new owner's standards. Similarly, reviewing staff roles and responsibilities can highlight opportunities for restructuring to better support the company's objectives. This assessment phase should be approached collaboratively, involving input from various departments to get a holistic view of the organization's needs and capabilities.

Setting up feedback channels is essential for making informed adjustments during the transition. Open feedback mechanisms encourage employees and customers to share their experiences and suggestions, fostering an inclusive culture. Establishing multiple feedback channels, such as anonymous suggestion boxes, regular surveys, and open-door policies, ensures everyone has a voice in the transition process.

Regularly reviewing and acting on feedback demonstrates a commitment to continuous improvement and inclusivity. For instance, if employees indicate through a survey that a particular process is causing bottlenecks, management can investigate and implement necessary changes.

Similarly, customer feedback about service delivery can guide improvements that enhance satisfaction and loyalty.

Building these feedback loops into the transition plan allows for flexibility and responsiveness, which are crucial for navigating the uncertainties of a post-acquisition phase. An inclusive approach not only improves decision-making but also strengthens the collective buy-in from all stakeholders, leading to more sustainable outcomes.

Final Thoughts

Navigating the final steps in purchasing a business involves careful preparation and clear communication to ensure a successful transition. In this chapter, we explored the essential documents required for closing a deal, including the Letter of Intent, Purchase Agreement, Closing Statement, and Transfer Documents. Each document serves a specific purpose, from laying the groundwork for negotiations to legally transferring ownership. Understanding these documents and ensuring their accuracy is crucial in protecting both parties' interests and paving the way for a smooth handover.

Effective management of the transition phase is equally important for maintaining operational stability and continuity. By developing a robust communication plan, engaging with staff and customers, assessing current operations, and setting up feedback channels, new owners can instill confidence and foster a positive working environment. These strategies not only help in minimizing disruptions but also build trust and loyalty among employees and clients. Through diligent preparation and thoughtful engagement, buyers can achieve a seamless transition, ensuring the newly acquired business thrives under its new ownership.

Chapter 9
Post-Purchase Integration

Post-purchase integration is essential for the seamless operation of a newly acquired business. Ensuring that both employees and clients adapt positively to changes requires strategic planning and execution. This chapter delves into effective onboarding practices that make employees feel welcomed and informed while maintaining clear communication with clients. By focusing on these aspects, businesses can ensure a smooth transition period.

Throughout the chapter, readers will explore how to create structured onboarding plans tailored specifically to new employees' needs, incorporating orientation programs and assigning mentors. Additionally, the importance of transparent client communication is emphasized, providing strategies for keeping clients informed and reassured during the ownership transition. The chapter also highlights organizing engaging training sessions for employees to align them with updated goals and standards, coupled with the use of feedback mechanisms to continuously improve the onboarding process. These strategies collectively contribute to achieving successful post-purchase integration in any business setting.

Onboarding Employees and Clients

Effective onboarding is crucial in ensuring that both employees and clients feel welcomed and informed during the transition period following a business acquisition. By cultivating a structured onboarding plan, establishing clear communication protocols with clients, organizing training sessions for employees, and implementing feedback mechanisms, a smooth post-purchase integration can be achieved.

Creating an Onboarding Plan is the first critical step in this process. A well-designed onboarding plan serves as a roadmap for new employees, outlining their roles, responsibilities, and expectations from the beginning. A detailed plan can help mitigate uncertainties and provide a clear direction, making it easier for employees to adapt to their new environment. This plan should incorporate resources like orientation programs, employee handbooks, and access to tools and technologies necessary for job performance. Additionally, assigning mentors or buddies to new hires can further support them through their initial days, providing personal guidance and fostering a sense of belonging within the team. Establishing a positive first impression through a comprehensive onboarding plan can lead to higher engagement and retention rates among employees.

Client Communication Protocols are equally important. Clients need to be informed about the change in ownership in a timely and transparent manner. Developing a strategy that utilizes various communication channels such as emails, newsletters, and face-to-face meetings ensures that all clients receive the information they need. Transparency about any potential changes to services or policies helps in maintaining client trust and loyalty. For instance, personalized communication where possible can make clients feel valued and understood. Updating the company's website and social media profiles to reflect new ownership can also serve as a proactive measure to keep clients in the loop. Providing reassurances about the continuity of service and addressing any concerns promptly can prevent misunderstandings and build a stronger relationship with clients.

Training Sessions for Employees play a pivotal role in introducing new processes or systems. Organizing these sessions not only enhances the competence and confidence of employees but also aligns them with the company's updated goals and standards. These training sessions should be interactive and engaging, allowing employees to ask questions and participate actively. Practical hands-on training, complemented by digital learning resources like webinars and instructional videos, can cater to different learning preferences. Regular follow-up sessions or refreshers ensure that the new knowledge is retained and applied effectively. Training also provides an opportunity for employees to network and collaborate, building a cohesive team that works together towards common objectives.

Feedback Mechanisms are essential to gauge the effectiveness of the onboarding process and identify areas for improvement. Implementing systems to gather feedback from both employees and clients enables leaders to make informed adjustments based on actual experiences. For employees, feedback can be collected through surveys, suggestion boxes, or one-on-one meetings. Creating an environment where employees feel comfortable sharing their thoughts without fear of repercussions fosters openness and continuous improvement. For clients, soliciting feedback through customer satisfaction surveys, focus groups, or direct communication helps in understanding their perspective and improving service delivery. Analyzing this feedback allows the organization to address any pain points proactively and enhance overall satisfaction.

Implementing these strategies requires careful planning and execution. Each component of the onboarding process is interconnected, contributing to the overall success of the integration. A structured onboarding plan ensures that employees have a clear understanding of their roles and are equipped with the necessary resources. Effective client communication protocols maintain transparency and trust, which are crucial for sustaining long-term relationships. Comprehensive training sessions empower employees with the skills and knowledge needed to excel in their roles. Feedback mechanisms provide valuable insights that guide continuous improvement and align the organization's practices with employee and client needs.

Implementing Operational Changes

Assessing Current Operations

Integrating a newly acquired business begins with establishing a clear understanding of its current operations. The first step is to conduct a comprehensive review of existing procedures, workflows, and systems. This evaluation will help identify areas that are functioning well and those that need improvement. Engaging both management and frontline employees in this process can yield valuable insights since they possess firsthand knowledge about the day-to-day operations.

Creating performance metrics is essential for assessing the efficiency and effectiveness of operations. These metrics provide a benchmark for comparing future performance and gauging improvements over time. Key performance indicators (KPIs) such as productivity rates, customer satisfaction scores, and financial metrics should be established. Employing data analytics tools can facilitate the collection and analysis of operational data, providing a clearer picture of where changes are needed.

Streamlining Processes

Once you have a thorough understanding of the current operations, it's time to identify processes that can be streamlined for greater efficiency. Streamlining involves simplifying workflows and eliminating unnecessary steps to save time and resources. It's vital to prioritize processes that have the highest impact on the organization's overall efficiency.

Utilizing technology solutions can significantly enhance process streamlining. Automation tools, for instance, can handle repetitive tasks, freeing up employees to focus on more strategic activities. Implementing software that integrates various functions, such as customer relationship management (CRM) and enterprise resource planning (ERP) systems, can also improve coordination and reduce redundancy.

Encouraging employee feedback during this phase is crucial. Employees who work directly with these processes may have practical suggestions for improvement. Creating open channels for communication and actively seeking input can foster a culture of continuous improvement. Regularly reviewing and refining processes based on employee feedback can lead to sustainable enhancements in operational efficiency.

Change Management Strategies

Implementing changes in an organization can be challenging, especially after an acquisition. Effective change management strategies are essential to ensure a smooth transition. Clear communication is at the heart of successful change management. Employees need to understand the rationale behind changes, how they will be affected, and what benefits the changes will bring to the organization.

Providing necessary training and resources is another critical component. Training sessions can equip employees with the skills and knowledge required to adapt to new processes and technologies. Continuous support through resources such as manuals, online courses, and helpdesks can ease the transition and build confidence among employees.

Building a coalition of leaders and influencers within the organization can also aid in driving change. These individuals can act as agents of change, advocating for the new initiatives and motivating their peers to embrace the changes. Recognizing and rewarding employees who exhibit adaptability and contribute positively to the integration process can further reinforce the desired behaviors.

Setting Performance Goals

Establishing clear performance goals is vital for steering the newly integrated business towards success. Goals provide direction and motivation, ensuring that everyone is working towards common objectives. Performance goals should be specific, measurable, achievable, relevant, and time-bound (SMART).

It's important to involve employees in the goal-setting process. When employees participate in setting their own goals, they are more likely to take ownership and feel committed to achieving them. Regularly revisiting and adjusting goals based on ongoing performance data is essential to keep them aligned with the organization's evolving needs and circumstances.

Performance benchmarks play a critical role in monitoring progress. Comparing actual performance against these benchmarks helps in identifying areas where additional support or adjustments are needed. Celebrating achievements and milestones can boost morale and encourage continued effort towards meeting performance goals.

Guideline for Implementation

1. **Comprehensive Review** : Start with a full assessment of the current operations to identify strengths and weaknesses. Use interviews and surveys with employees to gather diverse perspectives.
1. **Performance Metrics** : Establish KPIs that reflect critical aspects of business performance. Utilize data analytics tools for accurate measurement and reporting.
1. **Identifying Streamlining Opportunities** : Evaluate workflows to find redundant or cumbersome processes. Prioritize high-impact areas for immediate improvement.
1. **Technology Integration** : Implement technology solutions like CRM and ERP to facilitate better data flow and reduce manual efforts. Automate repetitive tasks wherever possible.
1. **Employee Feedback Mechanism** : Set up regular forums or suggestion boxes to collect employee feedback on processes. Actively involve employees in brainstorming and decision-making.
1. **Clear Communication Plan** : Develop a communication strategy that clearly explains the reasons for changes, benefits, and impacts on

employees. Use multiple channels to reach all stakeholders.

1. **Training Programs** : Design and conduct training sessions tailored to different employee needs, focusing on new processes, systems, and skills required for the transition.
1. **Leadership Coalition** : Identify and engage influential leaders and managers to champion the change initiatives within their teams, providing ongoing support and motivation.
1. **Setting SMART Goals** : Work with employees to set Specific, Measurable, Achievable, Relevant, and Time-bound performance goals. Ensure these goals align with organizational objectives.
1. **Regular Performance Reviews** : Schedule periodic reviews to assess progress against performance goals and KPIs. Adjust goals as necessary to reflect changing conditions and organizational priorities.
1. **Celebrate Successes** : Acknowledge and reward employee contributions and achievements throughout the integration process. Celebrate milestones to maintain enthusiasm and commitment.

Final Thoughts

Successfully acquiring a business is just the beginning; integrating it smoothly and ensuring that employees and clients adapt positively to the changes are crucial steps toward long-term success. This chapter provided strategies to help achieve this, starting with creating a structured onboarding plan for new employees. By outlining their roles and expectations from the start, you offer clarity and security. Moreover, establishing transparent client communication protocols ensures that your clients stay informed and continue to trust your services. Using various methods such as emails and personalized meetings guarantees comprehensive coverage, maintaining strong relationships during the transition.

Training sessions designed to introduce new processes or systems empower employees and align them with the company's updated goals. Interactive training fosters engagement and facilitates practical learning, while feedback mechanisms help you continuously refine the onboarding process. Gathering input from both employees and clients allows you to make necessary adjustments, fostering an environment of openness and continuous improvement. Implementing these strategies cohesively will ensure a smooth integration, enhancing overall satisfaction and setting a solid foundation for your newly acquired business to thrive.

Chapter 10
Case Studies and Success Stories

Examining case studies and success stories offers insightful learning opportunities for those looking to acquire a small business under $100,000. These real-world examples showcase the practical application of strategies and highlight common challenges faced during the acquisition process. By understanding the journeys of successful entrepreneurs, readers can gather valuable tips and inspiration for their own ventures.

In this chapter, we delve into the experiences of individuals who have navigated the complexities of purchasing a small business with limited budgets. The stories provide clear illustrations of effective market research, financial due diligence, and strategic negotiation. Readers will discover how these entrepreneurs identified potential risks, validated business models, and tailored their approaches to fit specific contexts. Additionally, the chapter explores the importance of continuous learning, operational efficiency, and creative marketing in driving business growth post-acquisition. Through these varied narratives, readers will gain a comprehensive understanding of what it takes to succeed in small business ownership.

Successful Acquisition Under $100K

John Thompson, an aspiring entrepreneur, had always harbored a dream of owning his own small business. When the opportunity arose to purchase a quaint coffee shop in his hometown, he saw the perfect chance to delve into the world of entrepreneurship. The coffee shop was a well-established fixture in the community, known for its cozy atmosphere and loyal customer base. Its reputation aligned perfectly with John's passion for both coffee and creating welcoming environments. The motivation behind this purchase was clear: John wanted to blend his personal interests with a profitable business venture.

As John embarked on the acquisition journey, he soon realized that identifying the right niche was just the beginning. His background in hospitality management helped him see the potential in the coffee shop, but he had to customize his strategies to fit the specific context of this business. Understanding the unique characteristics of the coffee shop, from its clientele to its location and existing operations, allowed him to tailor his approach effectively. This customization proved crucial to his success.

The acquisition process was a rigorous yet enlightening experience for John. He began by educating himself through various resources such as books, online courses, and seminars focused on small business acquisitions. He discovered that persistence in seeking educational materials and networking opportunities paid off greatly. Through local industry associations and online forums, John connected with seasoned entrepreneurs who provided valuable referrals and insights into businesses that were not publicly listed. This network became an invaluable asset, leading him to the coffee shop deal.

Patience and due diligence were cornerstones of John's acquisition strategy. He meticulously reviewed financial records, assessed the shop's performance, and scrutinized the lease agreement. This cautious approach ensured that there were no hidden surprises post-purchase. John also made several visits to the coffee shop, engaging with staff and customers to gather firsthand information. This thorough due diligence process not only protected his investment but also built his confidence in making informed decisions.

Despite the careful planning, John encountered several challenges during the buying process. Financing the purchase was a major hurdle; securing a loan required a convincing business plan and solid credit history. After facing initial rejections, John refined his pitch and provided detailed financial projections, eventually securing the necessary funds. Another challenge was negotiating favorable terms with the seller. This required flexibility and strong negotiation skills, as the seller was initially hesitant about some contract clauses. With patience and effective communication, they reached a mutually beneficial agreement.

The transition period after acquiring the coffee shop presented its own set of obstacles. Integrating new operational practices while maintaining the essence of what made the coffee shop beloved required a delicate balance. John faced resistance from long-term employees who were wary of change. However, by involving them in decision-making and clearly communicating his vision, he managed to build trust and foster a collaborative environment. Overcoming these challenges demonstrated John's resilience and ability to solve complex problems.

In the months following the acquisition, John implemented several growth strategies that significantly enhanced the business. He understood that creative marketing and customer engagement were vital for attracting new patrons and retaining existing ones. John leveraged social media platforms to create buzz around special promotions and community events hosted at the coffee shop. Collaborating with local artists and musicians for live performances transformed the venue into a cultural hub, drawing crowds and increasing customer loyalty.

Operational efficiencies were another area where John excelled. By analyzing workflow and identifying bottlenecks, he streamlined processes and reduced waste. Implementing a comprehensive staff training program improved service quality and consistency, further boosting customer satisfaction. These adaptations not only maximized profit margins but also instilled a sense of pride and ownership among employees.

Continuous learning and adaptation remained central to John's business philosophy. He regularly attended industry conferences and workshops to stay updated on market trends and best practices. This commitment to ongoing education allowed him to innovate and adapt to changing customer preferences. For instance, recognizing the trend towards healthier options, John expanded the menu to include organic and gluten-free products, meeting the demands of a diversifying customer base.

John's journey from acquisition to growth showcases the importance of strategic thinking and adaptability in the realm of small business ownership. His success story highlights several key takeaways for aspiring entrepreneurs. Customizing strategies to fit the specific business context is essential for achieving desired outcomes. Persistently seeking educational resources and leveraging networks can uncover hidden opportunities and provide critical support. Patience and meticulous due diligence protect investments and build confidence in decision-making.

Furthermore, resilience in the face of challenges shapes stronger, more capable entrepreneurs. Learning from setbacks enhances future decision-making, while problem-solving skills are indispensable for navigating complex transactions. Finally, continuous innovation and operational efficiency drive long-term growth and profitability. Creative marketing efforts and customer engagement can transform a business into a thriving community centerpiece.

Lessons Learned and Key Takeaways

Successful small business acquisitions under $100,000 are ripe with lessons that can illuminate the path for aspiring entrepreneurs. By examining real-world examples of successful acquisitions, we can distill valuable insights and strategies. One critical aspect of this process is thorough market research.

Market research is the cornerstone of any successful acquisition strategy. Understanding the market landscape helps in identifying potential businesses to purchase and assesses their viability. For instance, an entrepreneur interested in purchasing a local coffee shop must examine the competition, the demand for specialty coffee, and regional consumer preferences. Effective research not only highlights opportunities but also exposes hidden risks that might deter investment. For example, discovering that a particular area has a declining population or low foot traffic might suggest that investing in a retail outlet there could be risky.

Validation of the business model is another vital step. Entrepreneurs should delve into the current operational practices of the business they intend to acquire. Does the business have a sustainable and profitable model? Assessing past performance records, understanding revenue streams, and evaluating the customer base are essential. Without proper validation, jumping into a business acquisition is akin to taking a leap of faith. For instance, a boutique gym might have impressive membership numbers, but if those memberships are heavily discounted, the profitability might not be as sound as initially perceived.

Understanding customer demographics plays a pivotal role in tailoring services and products effectively. A business that keenly understands its customer base can cater to their specific needs better, ensuring sustained patronage and loyalty. If you're buying a children's toy store, knowing the age group, interests, and spending habits of parents in your area will help you stock the right items and design promotions that attract attention.

Financial acumen is indispensable when determining a fair valuation of the business. Financial due diligence entails scrutinizing balance sheets, income statements, cash flow records, and other financial documents to understand the true financial health of the business. For example, even a popular bakery could be a poor investment if it's carrying hefty debt or facing a sudden surge in overhead costs. Hence, buyers must be proficient in interpreting these financial documents to make informed decisions.

Moreover, being armed with financial literacy significantly bolsters one's negotiation position. When you understand the intricacies of financial statements, you can more effectively discuss terms and conditions. This literacy allows you to identify areas where adjustments might be necessary, such as negotiating a lower price based on discovered liabilities or securing extended payment terms to ease initial cash flow.

Awareness of potential hidden costs is crucial in preventing financial overextension. During the acquisition phase, it is essential to account for additional expenditures that might not be immediately apparent. These can include renovation costs, marketing expenses to attract new customers, or unexpected maintenance issues. Failure to consider these aspects can quickly inflate the acquisition cost and strain your finances. For instance, taking over a dated restaurant space without budgeting for essential renovations can lead to financial strain soon after the purchase.

Strong negotiation skills can dramatically influence the outcome of the acquisition process. Developing these skills involves understanding the seller's motivations, preparing thoroughly, and knowing when to stand firm or be flexible. Effective negotiators often secure favorable terms by building rapport with sellers. Establishing a positive relationship fosters open communication and goodwill, which can translate to better deal conditions. For example, a seller who feels comfortable and trusts you might be more willing to offer favorable financing terms or include valuable assets like equipment in the deal.

Negotiation isn't just about driving a hard bargain; it's about finding mutually beneficial solutions. Knowing when to be flexible can create win-win scenarios where both parties feel satisfied. If a seller needs a quick sale due to personal reasons, showing flexibility in the transaction timeline might earn you concessions elsewhere, such as a reduced sale price or additional inventory at no extra cost.

The journey doesn't end with the acquisition; post-purchase evaluation is essential for effective management. Continuous assessment of business performance helps identify areas requiring improvement. Regularly reviewing financial statements and operational metrics enables timely decision-making that can boost the business's success. Setting clear Key Performance Indicators (KPIs) provides measurable goals and keeps the team focused on achieving desired outcomes. For example, tracking monthly revenue, customer satisfaction scores, and employee productivity can highlight trends and pinpoint specific aspects needing attention.

Seeking feedback from customers and employees is invaluable for continuous enhancement. Customers provide firsthand insights into their experiences, while employees often have practical suggestions for improving operations. Implementing a feedback loop ensures ongoing improvements and helps maintain high standards. For instance, regular customer surveys might reveal a demand for new product lines, leading to strategic inventory expansion. Meanwhile, employee feedback could uncover process inefficiencies, guiding necessary operational changes.

Final Thoughts

In this chapter, we've delved into the journey of acquiring a small business for under $100,000, using John Thompson's experience as a guiding example.

His story highlights the importance of understanding the niche, conducting thorough market research, and validating the business model. Financial due diligence, persistence in learning, and leveraging networks are crucial steps that protect investments and open new opportunities. John's meticulous approach to reviewing financial records, engaging with staff and customers, and negotiating favorable terms showcases the critical elements necessary for a successful acquisition process.

Furthermore, John's post-acquisition strategies underline the significance of operational efficiencies and creative marketing. By fostering a collaborative environment and involving employees in decision-making, he managed to blend new practices with the coffee shop's cherished traditions. Continuous learning and adapting to market trends were key to his ongoing success, proving that resilience and innovation are vital for long-term growth. Aspiring entrepreneurs can draw valuable lessons from John's journey, understanding that strategic thinking and adaptability are the cornerstones of thriving in small business ownership.

Chapter 11
Ongoing Management and Growth

Managing and growing a newly acquired business requires a strategic approach that balances immediate operational needs with long-term growth objectives. This chapter, "Ongoing Management and Growth," offers readers practical tips and strategies to navigate this complex task. By focusing on continuous improvement, businesses can enhance their adaptability, foster innovation, and maintain a competitive edge in the market. Whether it's through implementing feedback loops or setting performance metrics, the strategies discussed will provide the essential tools needed for sustainable expansion.

Readers will find detailed methods for understanding customer and employee perspectives, which are crucial for identifying areas needing improvement. The chapter explores how to set actionable performance metrics that align with company goals and facilitate data-driven decisions. Additionally, it covers the adoption of lean principles to maximize efficiency and reduce waste in operations. Further discussions highlight the importance of investing in staff development to maintain a skilled and motivated workforce. By the end of this chapter, readers will have a comprehensive toolkit for driving continuous improvement and achieving sustainable growth in their newly acquired businesses.

Continuous Improvement Strategies

Enhancing business operations and customer satisfaction post-acquisition is critical for ensuring the long-term success of a newly acquired business. With continuous efforts in improvement, businesses can adapt to changing market conditions, foster innovation, and maintain a competitive edge. This section focuses on several strategies that will help achieve these goals: implementing feedback loops, setting performance metrics, adopting lean principles, and investing in staff development.

Implementing Feedback Loops

Implementing robust feedback loops is essential for understanding both customer and employee perspectives. Regularly gathering customer feedback provides valuable insights into their needs and expectations. This practice helps in swiftly identifying areas that require improvement, allowing businesses to address issues before they escalate. For example, a simple survey or comment card can reveal recurring complaints about product quality or service speed.

Acting on this feedback not only enhances customer satisfaction but also builds trust and loyalty.

Engaging employees in the feedback process is equally important. Employees often have firsthand knowledge of operational inefficiencies and customer pain points that management might overlook. By creating an open environment where employees feel comfortable sharing their thoughts, businesses can uncover opportunities for improvement that might otherwise go unnoticed. Moreover, involving employees in this process fosters a sense of ownership and commitment to the company's success. Regular team meetings, suggestion boxes, or anonymous surveys can be effective tools for collecting employee feedback.

The key to successful feedback loops is acting on the information gathered. Businesses should prioritize addressing the most critical issues first and communicate any changes made as a result of the feedback. This demonstrates to customers and employees that their input is valued and taken seriously, further encouraging ongoing participation in the feedback process.

Setting Performance Metrics

Setting clear, actionable performance metrics is another crucial element in managing and growing a business effectively. Key Performance Indicators (KPIs) provide measurable targets that guide the team's efforts and align them with the company's goals. For instance, a retail business might set KPIs such as sales growth, customer retention rate, and average transaction value. These metrics offer a concrete way to track progress and identify areas needing attention.

Regularly reviewing KPIs enables businesses to monitor performance trends and make data-driven decisions. If a KPI shows a downward trend, it signals a need for intervention before the issue affects overall performance. For example, if customer retention rates are falling, it might indicate problems with customer service or product offerings. Analyzing the underlying causes allows businesses to implement corrective actions promptly.

Performance metrics also foster accountability within the team. When employees know what is expected of them and understand how their performance is measured, they are more likely to stay focused and motivated. Clear KPIs help eliminate ambiguity, making it easier for everyone to contribute effectively towards the company's objectives. Regular performance reviews and discussions ensure that employees remain aligned with these goals and understand their role in achieving them.

Adopting Lean Principles

Adopting lean principles is a powerful strategy for enhancing efficiency and reducing waste in business operations. Lean practices focus on maximizing value while minimizing resources, which leads to significant cost savings and increased productivity. One key aspect of lean principles is the continuous evaluation of processes to identify and eliminate inefficiencies.

For example, a manufacturing company might analyze its production line to find steps that do not add value to the final product. By streamlining these processes, the company can reduce production time and costs while maintaining or improving product quality. Similarly, a service-oriented business could evaluate its customer service procedures to eliminate unnecessary steps that slow down response times.

Another fundamental principle of lean practices is fostering a culture of continuous improvement. Encouraging employees to regularly seek ways to enhance processes and reduce waste keeps the business agile and responsive to change. Implementing small, incremental changes can lead to substantial improvements over time. Tools such as value stream mapping, kaizen events, and the 5S methodology can help businesses systematically identify and address inefficiencies.

Moreover, lean principles emphasize the importance of empowering employees to take ownership of improvements. When employees are involved in problem-solving and decision-making, they are more invested in the outcome and more likely to sustain the changes. Training and supporting employees in lean methodologies ensure that everyone is equipped to contribute to the continuous improvement efforts.

Investing in Staff Development

Investing in staff development is vital for maintaining a skilled and motivated workforce. Providing training and development opportunities helps employees acquire new skills and improve existing ones, leading to enhanced service delivery and operational efficiency. For instance, a customer service team trained in advanced communication techniques will be better equipped to handle complex inquiries and resolve issues swiftly, resulting in higher customer satisfaction.

Continuous learning also prepares the business to adapt to industry changes and challenges. As technology evolves and markets shift, businesses must stay updated to remain competitive. Offering regular training programs, workshops, and access to professional development resources ensures that employees are well-prepared to navigate these changes. This proactive approach helps the business stay ahead of the curve and respond effectively to new opportunities and threats.

Furthermore, investing in staff development boosts employee morale and retention. When employees see that their employer is committed to their growth and career advancement, they are more likely to feel valued and loyal to the company. This reduces turnover rates and the associated costs of recruiting and training new hires. Programs such as mentorship, leadership training, and cross-functional projects can be particularly effective in developing employees' potential and preparing them for future roles within the organization.

Expanding Your Business Sustainably

Market Research for Growth Opportunities

To grow a business responsibly and sustainably, conducting thorough market research is paramount. Market research enables you to identify viable growth opportunities by understanding current trends and consumer needs. This foundation minimizes the risks associated with rapid expansion into new segments or regions. For example, if you own a retail store, researching customer preferences can reveal trending products or underserved markets. By meeting these demands, you create a strategic path for balanced growth.

Market research should be continuous rather than a one-time effort. Regularly gather data on your industry, competitors, and customers. Use surveys, focus groups, and online analytics to gain insights. These methods help build a comprehensive picture of where your business stands and what opportunities lie ahead. For instance, staying abreast of emerging technologies or changing consumer behaviors can position your business to capitalize on new avenues promptly.

Guideline: Conduct regular market research using various tools like surveys and online analytics to stay informed about industry trends, competitor activities, and customer preferences.

Developing a Scalable Business Model

A core component of sustainable growth is developing a scalable business model. Scalability means your business can expand without a proportional increase in costs. This requires creating replicable systems and streamlined operational processes that manage larger volumes efficiently. Take the example of a tech company; developing software that can handle an increasing number of users without requiring additional infrastructure exemplifies scalability.

To achieve this, start by evaluating your existing processes. Identify areas where automation or streamlined workflows can reduce bottlenecks. A scalable model often relies on technology to support growth. Implementing cloud computing solutions or customer relationship management (CRM) systems can be instrumental. For instance, automating customer service through chatbots can handle increased inquiries without needing more staff.

Guideline: Create scalable systems by streamlining operations and leveraging technology to allow growth without significant cost increases.

Building Strategic Partnerships

Engaging in strategic partnerships offers another pathway to responsible growth. Collaborations with other businesses can unlock new markets and resources that would otherwise be inaccessible. For example, partnering with a logistics firm can enhance your distribution capabilities without the need to invest heavily in infrastructure. Such alliances not only broaden your reach but also lend credibility to your brand.

Choosing the right partners is crucial. Look for businesses that complement your services or products. Shared values and goals ensure a more harmonious partnership. Consider entering co-branding agreements or joint ventures that benefit both parties. For instance, a local coffee shop could partner with a bakery to offer exclusive products, thereby attracting customers from both businesses.

Guideline: Engage with complementary businesses to explore collaborative growth opportunities that expand your market reach and resource access.

Prioritizing Financial Health

Lastly, ensuring that your growth plans are underpinned by solid financial strategies is critical. Sound financial management protects against overextending, which can jeopardize your business's viability. Begin by creating a detailed budget that outlines your growth expenses and anticipated revenues. This budget serves as a roadmap, helping you allocate resources efficiently.

Regularly review your financial performance to make informed decisions about investments. Monitor key financial metrics such as cash flow, profit margins, and return on investment. For instance, if you're considering expanding your product line, assess the potential profitability versus the initial costs involved. Financial health isn't just about avoiding debt; it's about making strategic investments that drive long-term value.

Guideline: Ensure all growth initiatives are backed by careful financial planning and regular performance reviews to avoid overextension and maintain viability.

Final Thoughts

This chapter has provided you with a practical toolkit for managing and growing your newly acquired business. By implementing feedback loops, setting clear performance metrics, adopting lean principles, and investing in staff development, you can create a robust system for continuous improvement. These strategies are essential for staying competitive, enhancing operational efficiency, and boosting both employee and customer satisfaction. Remember, the key is to act on what you learn from feedback, continuously refine your processes, and ensure that your team is engaged and well-trained.

Looking ahead, embrace these strategies as part of your daily operations to drive sustainable growth. Continuously seek out opportunities for improvement and innovation, and make data-driven decisions based on your established performance metrics. Foster a culture where everyone feels invested in the success of the business, and never underestimate the power of a well-trained, motivated workforce. With these tools at your disposal, you're well-equipped to navigate the challenges and seize the opportunities that come with managing your new business.

Chapter 12
Conclusion

Achieving a successful business acquisition involves revisiting the journey you've undertaken and solidifying your next steps. This chapter will guide you through reflecting on the critical phases of your acquisition process, emphasizing the importance of each stage in contributing to your overall success. By reinforcing the knowledge you've already gained, this chapter aims to boost your confidence and equip you with actionable steps that can transform your theoretical understanding into practical success.

We'll delve into key aspects like identifying viable businesses, conducting comprehensive due diligence, and negotiating favorable terms. Furthermore, we'll discuss how to smoothly transition ownership and manage post-purchase integration for sustained growth. Each section is designed to provide you with clear, actionable insights, ensuring you're well-prepared to navigate the complexities of acquiring and managing a new business with optimism and strategic foresight.

Recap of the Journey and Emphasizing Due Diligence

Acquiring a business is a complex journey that requires careful planning and execution. As we reach the conclusion of this book, it is crucial to revisit the key steps in the business acquisition process and understand why each stage is vital for achieving successful ownership. By reflecting on these steps, you can reinforce your knowledge and feel more confident in your ability to navigate the acquisition landscape.

The first step in the acquisition process is identifying viable businesses. This involves conducting market research to pinpoint industries and companies that match your investment criteria and align with your long-term goals. It's essential to assess factors such as market trends, competitive landscape, and growth potential. Selecting the right target sets the foundation for a successful acquisition and helps you avoid investing in a business with inherent risks that could hinder your objectives.

Once you've identified potential targets, the next step is conducting thorough due diligence. Due diligence is the process of investigating the financial, legal, operational, and strategic aspects of the target business. This step is critical because it provides a comprehensive understanding of the business's true value and potential risks. It ensures that you are making informed decisions based on accurate and complete information. By examining financial statements, contracts, customer relationships, and compliance records, due diligence helps safeguard against unforeseen liabilities and identifies opportunities for improvement post-acquisition.

In the due diligence phase, it's important to pay particular attention to financial analysis. Evaluating financial health involves scrutinizing profit and loss statements, balance sheets, and cash flow statements. Understanding the financial performance of the business allows you to verify its profitability, assess working capital needs, and forecast future revenue streams. A detailed financial analysis also uncovers any red flags, such as outstanding debts or irregularities in financial reporting, which could impact the viability of the acquisition.

Legal due diligence is equally important. This involves reviewing all legal documents, including corporate records, employment agreements, intellectual property registrations, and ongoing litigation. Ensuring compliance with laws and regulations protects you from inheriting legal issues that could result in fines or damage the business's reputation. Additionally, understanding contractual obligations with suppliers, customers, and partners is vital to avoid disruptions in business operations post-acquisition.

Operational due diligence focuses on the day-to-day functioning of the business. This includes evaluating the efficiency of business processes, assessing the quality of the workforce, and examining supply chain management. Identifying strengths and weaknesses in operations enables you to implement improvements that enhance productivity and reduce costs. For instance, if the target business has outdated technology, upgrading systems can lead to better data management and streamlined operations.

Strategic due diligence looks at the alignment between the target business and your overall vision. This step assesses the strategic fit by considering factors such as market position, brand value, and synergies with your existing operations. Understanding how the acquisition will integrate with your current business structure and how it will contribute to your growth strategy ensures that the purchase aligns with your long-term objectives.

After completing due diligence, the next step is negotiating the terms of the acquisition. Negotiation involves reaching an agreement on the purchase price, payment structure, and other conditions of the sale. Effective negotiation is crucial because it determines the financial implications and outlines the responsibilities of both parties. Striking a fair deal requires balancing your interests with those of the seller, ensuring that the terms provide value while mitigating potential risks.

Once the acquisition agreement is finalized, the focus shifts to closing the deal and transferring ownership. This stage encompasses completing all legal paperwork, securing financing, and formalizing the transfer of assets. It's essential to manage this transition smoothly to maintain business continuity and preserve employee morale. Clear communication with stakeholders, including employees, customers, and suppliers, ensures that they are informed about the changes and reassured about the future direction of the business.

Post-purchase management is the final, yet ongoing, stage of the acquisition process. Successfully integrating the acquired business into your operations is key to realizing the benefits of the acquisition. This involves aligning corporate cultures, consolidating operations, and implementing strategic initiatives to drive growth. Continuous monitoring and evaluation of performance against set objectives help identify areas for improvement and ensure that the business remains on track to meet its goals.

Effective post-purchase management requires strong leadership and a clear vision. Engaging with employees and fostering a collaborative environment promotes a sense of unity and shared purpose. Providing training and development opportunities enhances skills and motivates the workforce to contribute to the company's success. Additionally, maintaining transparent communication channels with all stakeholders builds trust and supports smooth integration.

The role of due diligence as a critical safeguard cannot be overemphasized. Thorough due diligence acts as a shield, protecting you from potential pitfalls and enabling you to make informed decisions. By meticulously analyzing all aspects of the target business, you minimize risks and maximize the likelihood of a successful acquisition. It prevents costly mistakes, such as overpaying for a business or inheriting unexpected liabilities, which could jeopardize your investment.

To illustrate the importance of due diligence, consider the case of a company acquiring a manufacturing firm. Without proper due diligence, the acquiring company might overlook hidden environmental liabilities associated with the manufacturing processes. These liabilities could result in significant cleanup costs and regulatory penalties, severely impacting the financial stability of the newly acquired business. However, with comprehensive due diligence, these issues would be identified early, allowing for renegotiation of terms or even reconsideration of the acquisition altogether.

Similarly, due diligence ensures that you are aware of any potential challenges related to intellectual property rights. For example, if the target business relies heavily on proprietary technology, verifying the validity and enforceability of patents and trademarks is crucial. Undiscovered intellectual property disputes could lead to costly legal battles and disrupt business operations. Conducting thorough due diligence mitigates these risks, providing peace of mind and a solid foundation for future growth.

Real-World Application and Long-Term Vision

Applying the insights you've gained in this book into real-world scenarios is crucial for achieving success as a business owner. It's not just about knowing the concepts; it's also about implementing them effectively. Imagine taking the strategies and knowledge we've discussed and using them to navigate your business acquisition journey. It's like building a bridge from theoretical understanding to practical application. This approach will help you to transform potential obstacles into opportunities for growth.

To see tangible results, you need to be proactive in applying what you've learned. Think of each insight as a tool in your toolkit, ready to be used when needed. For instance, if you've learned about effective negotiation tactics, try applying those techniques in your next business deal. By doing so, you'll not only sharpen your skills but also increase your chances of securing favorable terms. Remember, the application of knowledge is the cornerstone of success. Without taking action, even the most profound insights remain dormant and ineffective.

Consider long-term growth as a lighthouse guiding your journey beyond the initial acquisition. Often, new business owners focus heavily on the first steps of purchasing a business, overlooking what comes next. While the initial phase is undoubtedly significant, true success lies in your ability to sustain and grow the business over time. Envision where you want your business to be in five, ten, or even twenty years. What steps can you take today to ensure that future vision becomes a reality? By setting long-term goals and devising strategies to achieve them, you align your daily actions with your ultimate aspirations, ensuring a steady progression towards sustained success.

Effective management and strategic planning are key components in driving long-term business growth. Effective management involves not just overseeing day-to-day operations but also being adaptable and responsive to changes in the market. A well-managed business can pivot when necessary, taking advantage of new opportunities while mitigating risks. For example, consider how technological advancements could impact your operations. Staying updated with industry trends and incorporating relevant innovations into your business model can give you a competitive edge, fostering continuous improvement and growth.

Strategic planning, on the other hand, is about setting clear objectives and outlining the steps required to achieve them. It's essential to revisit and revise your strategies regularly, ensuring they remain relevant and aligned with your long-term goals. A flexible strategy allows you to adjust your course as needed, keeping your business on track despite any unforeseen challenges. Think of your strategic plan as a living document that evolves with your business. By continually refining your strategies, you maintain momentum and adaptability, both of which are crucial for sustained success.

Incorporating a guideline here, it's beneficial to periodically assess your business's performance against your long-term goals. Establish key performance indicators (KPIs) that reflect your objectives and measure progress consistently. Regular assessments provide valuable insights into what's working and what needs adjustment, helping you stay aligned with your growth aspirations. This disciplined approach ensures that your actions are continuously directed towards achieving your long-term vision.

It's also valuable to surround yourself with a strong support network. Mentorship, peer groups, and professional advisors can offer fresh perspectives and invaluable advice. Engaging with others who have navigated similar paths can provide you with the encouragement and guidance you need to overcome challenges. Their experiences can serve as lessons, helping you to avoid common pitfalls and seize opportunities more effectively. Building and nurturing these relationships can significantly enhance your ability to manage and grow your business successfully.

Furthermore, investing in your development and the development of your team is crucial. Continuous learning and skill development keep you and your team prepared to handle emerging challenges and capitalize on new opportunities. Attend workshops, seminars, and networking events to stay informed and inspired. Encourage your team to pursue professional development courses that align with their roles and the company's goals. A well-informed and skilled team is an asset, driving innovation and efficiency within the organization.

Another essential aspect of long-term growth is financial management. Maintaining a healthy cash flow and effectively managing your finances ensures that you have the resources needed to invest in growth opportunities. Develop a robust financial plan that includes budgeting, forecasting, and regular financial reviews. This disciplined approach helps you anticipate future needs and make informed decisions, supporting sustainable growth.

As we look at the broader picture, let's reinforce the idea that patience and perseverance are vital traits for any successful business owner. Growth doesn't happen overnight; it requires consistent effort and resilience. There will be times when progress seems slow or challenges appear insurmountable. During such periods, maintaining a positive mindset and staying committed to your long-term goals is crucial. Remember why you started this journey and let that drive propel you forward.

Guidelines play an important role in ensuring consistent quality and performance within your business. Establish standard operating procedures (SOPs) that outline best practices for various tasks and processes. These guidelines provide your team with clear instructions, reducing variability and enhancing efficiency. Regularly review and update these SOPs to reflect new insights and improvements, ensuring they continue to support your long-term objectives.

Finally, celebrate your successes along the way. Acknowledging and rewarding achievements boosts morale and keeps motivation high. Whether it's hitting a financial milestone, launching a new product, or improving customer satisfaction, take time to appreciate the effort and dedication that led to these accomplishments. Celebrations foster a positive work environment and create a sense of shared purpose among your team, reinforcing their commitment to the collective goals. By recognizing and valuing progress, you cultivate a culture of success that drives your business forward.

Bringing It All Together

Reflecting on the comprehensive journey of acquiring a business, it's clear that each stage plays a crucial role in paving the path to successful ownership. From identifying viable targets and conducting meticulous due diligence to negotiating favorable terms and managing post-purchase integration, every step demands attention and strategic effort. By applying the knowledge shared in this chapter, you can confidently navigate these stages, avoiding potential pitfalls and seizing growth opportunities. The emphasis on thorough due diligence, in particular, stands out as a shield that safeguards your investment and ensures informed decision-making.

Looking ahead, the true measure of success lies in not just acquiring a business but also sustaining and growing it over time. This requires proactive application of insights, effective management, and strategic planning. Fostering a strong support network and investing in continuous learning are key components of long-term growth. By setting clear goals, regularly assessing performance, and maintaining financial discipline, you create a roadmap for sustained success. Remember, patience and perseverance are vital; celebrate achievements along the way to keep morale high and motivation strong. By embracing these principles, you're well-prepared to turn your business acquisition into a thriving enterprise.

www.ingramcontent.com/pod-product-compliance
Lightning Source LLC
Chambersburg PA
CBHW070147230526
45471CB00002B/559